ERIC, A WAIF
A Story of Last Century

Nadakkavu, Kozhikode, Kerala, 673011
www.insightpublica.com
e-mail: insightpublica@gmail.com

Title: **ERIC, A WAIF A Story of Last Century**
Author: **EMMA LESLIE**
First Insight Edition: August 2024

Printed and Published by
InsightinPublica Printers & Publishers Pvt. Ltd.
ISBN: 978-93-5517-504-5

ERIC, A WAIF

A Story of Last Century

EMMA LESLIE

INSIGHT PUBLICA®

contents

CHAPTER I.

ERIC HUNTER.

"SO the old witch is dead, and Dame Willoughby may hope to raise a whole brood of chickens, and Farmer Sawyer need not fear his cheese will be spoiled;" and the speaker lifted his broad-brimmed tattered hat, and wiped the perspiration from his brow, looking expectantly at the landlord of The Magpie as he did so.

"That news is worth a horn of ale, isn't it, Master Tyler?" he asked, when he found it met with little response.

"Humph! The news might have been better, and it might have been worse. The poor woman was a stranger in these parts, I'll allow, but that was all that could be proved against her. Where's the boy?" added the landlord, with a little more interest.

"Him they call Eric? Did ever an English-born lad have such a name as that?" said the other in a grumbling tone, as he slowly raised the horn of ale to his lips before answering the landlord's question. "He'll be up there with his mother, I suppose; the two were always together."

"Poor little chap, he'll find the world a hard place, I'm afraid, now his mother has gone."

"Serve 'em right. They should ha' bided in their own parish, and not come poking their noses where they wasn't wanted," said the other.

The landlord made no reply to this, for he knew the man did but express the sentiment of the whole neighbourhood in the words he had spoken.

Summerleigh was a quiet, self-contained little village on the edge of Epping Forest, far enough from London to be very jealous of the intrusion of strangers if they stayed more than a night at the inn, unless they happened to be visitors at the Hall. So when the poor woman came with her only son, a lad of ten, to occupy the little cottage that had stood tenantless so long on the edge of the forest clearing, the whole parish was stirred to discover who she was and why she came there.

She said herself that it was for the fresh air of the forest; but nobody believed this, any more than they believed that fresh air made any difference to people's health; they chose to believe any but this simple reason for seeking a home in their locality.

They soon discovered that she was poor, but industrious, for mother and son worked in the garden early and late, selling the herbs they raised, and also salves and lotions made from them, until the rumour spread somehow, that the knowledge she possessed of the healing qualities of herbs and simples growing about the forest had not been gained by any good means. In other words, she was a witch, and people professed to be afraid of buying her salves.

Then another overheard her singing a hymn one day to the hum of her spinning-wheel as she sat at work, and this was held to be proof that she was a Methodist, which was quite as bad as being a witch, and equally punishable by law, at the time of which we write.

That Mrs. Hunter had not sought to make friends among her gossiping neighbours was sufficient for either or both of these charges to be deemed capable of proof, by those who openly declared they hated all strangers, so that it was not wonderful that she lived an isolated life. That she did not mind this, but seemed to find her boy Eric an all-sufficient companion and friend, was another wonder to Summerleigh, and one it bitterly resented; for there was small scope for persecuting a woman so independent as Mrs. Hunter, especially as they were glad to buy her herbs, because they could not get them so good anywhere else.

How long the poor woman had been ill before she died, none seemed to know. The landlord of The Magpie asked several of his customers who dropped in during the evening, but none seemed to know anything about it, or had troubled to inquire. All seemed to know of her death, but nothing beyond this fact.

When closing time came, John Tyler made a great business of looking over the stables before shutting them, and when he went back to the inn parlour, where his wife was waiting for him to go up to bed, he said, "If old Toby don't soon come back, I shall have to get somebody else to look after things out there."

"I should think so, indeed," said Mrs. Tyler tartly. "You might have looked after somebody else a month ago. When are you coming upstairs?" she added, as he turned to secure the wooden latch of the door.

There was no more said that night, but the next morning, when Tyler was dressing himself, he remarked, in a casual way, "I think I shall get a boy to take old Toby's place."

His wife laughed. "So you've come to my way of thinking at last, John Tyler," she said, as she briskly tied the strings of her white muslin cap before going downstairs.

Eric Hunter's name had not been mentioned; but that was the lad Tyler had in his mind when he spoke to his wife. And after breakfast, he went across the garden and orchard, and out into the forest road, for that was the nearest way to the widow's cottage, and he had made up his mind to see Eric at once and conclude the business, for fear another village lad should come after the place.

Eric was fourteen now, a tall, sturdy lad, strong and healthy, in spite of his refined face, that flushed crimson when he opened the door and saw the landlord of The Magpie standing on the step.

"Mother is dead, sir," he said, in a quiet, weary tone, as though it was an everyday fact he was speaking of.

"Yes, my boy, I heard about it yesterday, and I thought I would just step up and see if things had been put comfortable for her." And there the landlord stopped, and gazed round the little bare room.

The widow's spinning-wheel stood in one corner, a small deal table in the centre, and two rush-bottomed chairs were placed back against the wall, but all was scrupulously clean and neat.

"I've done everything that mother told me, you will see, sir." And the boy led the way into an inner room, and there, in the dim light, Tyler saw the outlined figure of the poor woman, with a sheet carefully drawn over it. "Mother told me I was to do that, and then wait until God sent help to me, and I've been waiting, only somehow it seemed a long time. Did God send you, sir?" asked the boy, as though he had expected a less commonplace messenger than the landlord of The Magpie.

The question evidently puzzled the man a good deal, for God was not in all his thoughts, as He was in Eric's; but the sight of the clean, tidy home made him think Eric would make an excellent ostler, and so he said, as he scratched his head thoughtfully, "I don't understand much about parson's work; I've got enough to do to mind The Magpie and please The Magpie's missis, and so I've come to see if you'd lend a hand in the stable, as Toby don't seem likely to get better yet awhile."

Eric was a little puzzled, but at last he said, "Do you mean me to help with the horses, sir?"

"To be sure I do; that's what I've come to see you about, my lad," replied Tyler, with another look round the room.

"Thank you, sir," answered the boy eagerly; "I've always loved horses, and wanted to have something to do with them. Mother said if it was good for me to be with the beasts, God would let me do it some day; so that I am sure God sent you, though you may not quite understand it, any more than I do."

"Then you'll come to The Magpie?" said Tyler.

"Oh yes, sir, and thank you; but—but—didn't God say anything about burying mother?" added the boy in a changed tone, the tears filling his eyes, though he tried to wink them away, for fear his visitor should see them.

"Hasn't anybody been to see about that? Haven't you got any friends or relatives?" exclaimed the landlord in a helpless tone.

"No, sir; there's only mother and me. The doctor came to see her last week, and he told me when he went away that she couldn't live long, and yesterday she said she was going home to God, and I should have to stay here a bit without her." And again the tears rose to his eyes, in spite of all his efforts to keep them back.

"Bless me, somebody must come and see about the business for you," interrupted his visitor; and he turned away to go to the parish clerk, who lived at the other end of the village, nearly two miles off.

When he got home about an hour later, it was to hear that old Toby had hobbled out to resume his work. Some rumour had reached him of a boy being engaged to do this for the future, which made the old fellow decide that he could "look after things in the stable" once more; and so the landlord was met with the news of his return as soon as he got back.

"It's lucky you hadn't engaged a boy," said Mrs. Tyler, looking keenly at her husband as she spoke; "for if you had, there's no telling but what you might think of keeping the two, soft as you are; but I asked Marple if you had been after his Jack."

"I should want a boy a long time before I took Jack Marple," interrupted Tyler, with some spirit; "but all the same, I have engaged a boy. Widow Hunter's son is a decent lad."

"The witch-wife's boy?" almost screamed Mrs. Tyler.

"Nobody can prove she was a witch, any more than they can prove she was a Methodist," said Tyler angrily. Though, as he thought of Eric's talk, he feared the latter charge would be easy enough of proof, and he decided to give the boy a word of warning to keep all such thoughts to himself for the future.

Fortunately for the landlord, customers arrived the next minute, and so he left his wife to exhaust her grumbling on Betty, while he went to the cellar to draw the cider that had been called for, and to ascertain whether the visitors who had just alighted from a post-chaise would want dinner prepared for them.

That his services should be required so soon was a real grievance to old Toby, who had seated himself in a sunny corner of the gateway, with a fixed determination that he would not move again until he went home at night, when this obnoxious chaise arrived; and the occupants were so inconsiderate as to say that they were going to spend some hours in the forest, and would want the horse fed and rubbed down, and the chaise looked over, as one wheel had sunk in the rutty road rather deeper than usual.

To hear the old man's grumbling maledictions on all strangers who came to Summerleigh annoyed the landlord, and seeing Eric pass down the road, he called to him.

"Are you busy just now, my lad?" he said, when Eric came up.

"No; I'm only going to see if parson is at home, to tell him about mother," he replied.

"Well, I can tell you that parson went to London three days ago, and won't be back for another week; but Mr. Jackson is going to see about your mother's funeral. He is a friend of mine," added Tyler.

"Thank you, sir. Can I do anything for you now?" said Eric, with a glance towards the stable-yard.

"Yes—no—I've visitors, and old Toby is in the stable; but—"

"You would like me to help Toby with the horse?" said Eric eagerly.

"That's just about it, my lad; but I'm not sure how he'll take your help."

Eric did not wait to hear more, but ran down the stable-yard to where the old man was fumbling with the buckles of the harness, and swearing at the horse, which was impatient to get out of the shafts and into the cool stable.

"Here, you boy, just come here and undo this," called the old man when he heard Eric approaching; "they don't know how to make straps now; every man seems to forget how things ought to be done," he grumbled, as he seated himself on an upturned bucket to superintend the cleaning and feeding of the horse; for, as Eric had proved himself handy in unfastening the buckles, the old man set him to feed the horse, and then to rub it down before leading it to the stable for a rest.

Eric took a real interest in his work, patting the horse and stroking him as he slowly munched his food, and rubbing him down with as gentle a touch as possible, so that Toby, finding his work done so well for him, was disposed to be civil to the boy, until just as the work was over, he discovered who he was. Then he burst into a storm of passionate protests against all strangers, be they witches or Methodists, declaring that he believed he was himself bewitched by the boy to let him do this work for him.

"That's all very well, Toby," said the landlord, who had stepped outside to see how Eric was getting on; "you take good care not to find fault until the work is done. Ah, and well done, too," said the master, as he slowly walked round the horse and surveyed it with a critical eye.

"Send him away, master, send him away!" foamed old Toby, hobbling to his feet, and trying to seize Eric.

"Now go and sit down, and be reasonable, Toby, and we may be able to settle this matter without any fuss. Before you came back this morning, I had arranged with this lad that he should come and help me in the stable."

"Don't you think I would save you from it, master?" said old Toby imploringly. "Remember what his mother was—a witch woman, if ever there was one. Don't you think old Toby would save you from that, master?" And there was no doubt of the old man being genuinely concerned for his master's welfare.

"Now look here, that talk about Mrs. Hunter being a witch is all moonshine, and I mean to give the lad a trial here in the stable. If you choose to come back and overlook things for me, well and good; but if you won't work with the lad fairly and squarely, as an Englishman should, then say so at once, and I shall know what to be about."

"Why, master, he's bewitched you as well as me," said the old fellow complainingly.

"Very well; if you think that, keep away from The Magpie for the future, and we will manage the stables by ourselves without your help," said the landlord.

But this did not at all suit old Toby, much as he might dislike Eric, and even fear him, as he doubtless did; for to lose his occupation entirely would never do; so he went back to his seat grumbling about new men and new ways; which the landlord understood well enough as a slight reminder that he could not boast of being born in Summerleigh, as Toby himself could.

The landlord did not wish old Toby to give up his post as ostler of The Magpie. It would pay him much better to keep old Toby, and to have Eric to do his work, for Toby by himself drove customers away, but since he had come back, it would not do to let him say he would not work with Eric; so that the landlord was quite as much disposed to settle the matter in a friendly fashion as the old ostler was.

So, while Eric was set to sweep up the stable and yard, Tyler talked to the old man, and at last it was settled that he should come every day and overlook the affairs of the stables, while Eric was to do the actual work, and get his food from the kitchen, which, with occasional tips from customers, would be considered remuneration enough—at least for the present.

CHAPTER II

AT THE MAGPIE

ERIC HUNTER'S quiet life had made him thoughtful beyond his years, and old Toby's invectives, while they did not surprise him very much, awoke once more the fears that had tortured him ever since the doctor had told him his mother could not live long.

But he bravely kept back the tears of grief and dismay, and went on with his task of sweeping up the stable-yard, while old Toby and the landlord adjusted their quarrel over him.

He longed to say, "I will not stay in this place to hear my mother called a witch;" but she had made him promise that if he could possibly get employment in Summerleigh, he would not venture into the world beyond, until he was older. And so, for this promise sake, he held his peace.

Before he went home in the evening, the landlord contrived to give him half a rye loaf and a bottle of cider for his supper; but, though he was hungry and faint, the boy could not eat just yet.

Going into the inner room, where all that he could see of his mother still lay, he threw himself on his knees beside the bed, and sobbed out his grief and fears for the future.

"Oh, mother, mother!" he sobbed. "Let me go away from this place; I can never stop here. Anything would be better than stopping here with that old Toby for a master. Let me find my way to London, and try to get work there. I have waited as you told me for God to send a messenger to help me, but nobody has come but the landlord of The Magpie, and surely he wasn't God's messenger—he can't help me much."

It was a relief to the boy to pour out his grief and fear and doubt in this fashion, but he had no intention of breaking his promise; and hard as it was to think that Tyler could be the expected messenger of mercy who was to come and help him out of his difficulties, he had no intention of breaking away from the engagement he had made to work in the stable under old Toby.

But he grew calmer and more content before he rose from his knees; and as he folded back the sheet to look at the waxen face that lay beneath, he whispered once more, "I will keep my promise, mother, and stay here as long as I can."

He heard the next day that arrangements had been made for the funeral, but it would cost all the money their poor furniture would fetch to pay for it, and the owner of the cottage wanted that for another tenant by the end of the week, so that before Sunday, Eric would be homeless as well as motherless.

This was a difficulty the landlord had not foreseen when he engaged him to help Toby, but it did not make him the less determined to befriend the lad, although his wife saw in it a reason for sending him before the justice of the peace, to have him transported as a beggar, and thus rid Summerleigh of him for ever.

"There's no occasion for that," said her husband quickly; "the boy is not a beggar, and never likely to become one, unless he is driven to it. Remember you were left motherless, and might have shared a similar fate, if my mother had not taken pity on you." And with this timely reminder, that never failed to bring Mrs. Tyler to reason, the landlord left her, to think out for himself a plan of lodging Eric.

Fortunately there was plenty of room in the numerous outhouses in the stable-yard, and at last it was settled that he should bring his little box, that contained his few clothes and some letters that his mother had told him to keep, and put it in the hayloft, where he could sleep.

It was a rough lodging, but in those times, boys were used to rough treatment generally, and so he had little cause to complain. Old Toby grumbled and found fault continually, but Eric soon began to learn that the master's eye was upon him, and if he took pains with a visitor's horse, though Toby might pocket the gratuity that should of right have been his, the landlord often gave him a kind word or look of appreciation that was worth more than money to him.

Betty and her mistress were by no means friendly to him for some time. They professed to be afraid of him, to see something in his eyes that told of his witch parentage, and they often kept him waiting for his meals, if the master was not about to see that he had his food given to him at the proper time.

But although old Toby was cross and suspicious, and seldom gave him a kind word, the old man was so fond of airing his knowledge of horses and their ways and ailments, that Eric could not fail to learn a good deal from him, although he was careful to keep this knowledge to himself, and never attempt the expression of an opinion upon anything, whatever he might think upon the matter.

There were a few post-horses owned by the landlord, and these soon learned to know and welcome the lad when he went into the stable; for he often saved a morsel of bread from his own meal as a dainty for them, and when they came back from a journey, tired and over-driven, as they often did, he contrived to rub them with some lotion his mother had taught him how to make from herbs growing in the forest, the secret of which he kept to himself; for old Toby would be sure to object to its use if he found it out, and he was not sure that his master might not fear he was trying to hurt the poor brutes instead of helping them.

His love for these dumb friends, and the liberty that he had to show his love to them in his own way, was almost his only comfort in life now; for he was never allowed to forget that his mother was under the ban of suspicion, and that he shared it.

There were a good many hours in the course of a week when he was not wanted at all about the stables; and as Betty disdained receiving any help from him in her kitchen work, he was left free to roam about the forest almost as he had done during his mother's life. To search for herbs and roots to make his lotions and salves for the horses, and watch the ways and habits of the creatures who lived among its thickets, became the pastime of his life, since he was denied human friendship. Here, too, he found comfort and solace for his grief, and at last began to hope that there might be a place for him in the world after all.

"If I could only hope there was room for me somewhere, that I was of use to somebody, it would be something to live for," he would whisper to himself; for he had been told more than once by Toby and Betty too that his master had only taken him out of charity, and not at all because he wanted him, so that Eric might be excused for thinking there was no room for him in this great busy world that God had made, but which man seemed to manage so badly.

His master had given him a word of warning about speaking to Toby or anybody else as he had to him when he first went to the cottage.

"If you were to speak to Toby about God caring for you, as you seem to think He does, he would be sure to say you were one of these Methodists who are turning the world upside down; and much as I might want to help you, I couldn't do it, for parson and squire too are both dead against the Methodists, and I should lose my licence if it was thought I harboured one of these pestilent people about The Magpie stables. Not that I think you are a Methodist," the landlord hastened to add; "but you see I couldn't have a fuss here, as there would be if anybody heard you talk as I did."

"Thank you, sir; I'll remember what you say," replied Eric; but he sighed as he spoke, for he had been used to talk to his mother quite freely about these matters, and she had taught him to believe in God as a very present help in every time of trouble—a Friend who would never fail to help the helpless, and who loved to have His children seek that help and talk about it among themselves.

To be debarred from speaking of what had grown to be a part of his very life was not easy therefore to Eric, who had been taught to connect God with every portion of it, and to believe that the small events, as well as the larger and more important ones, were under the guiding hand of Him who had promised to lead and guide His children every step of their way.

Being thus thrown upon himself, it was not strange that, as the months passed, and he grew more accustomed to the work in the stable, and consequently able to do it quicker, he should betake himself to the forest more frequently, making friends with its furred and feathered inhabitants, and enjoying the society of those who would trust themselves to him. He never sought to entrap them or make prisoners of them longer than they desired to stay near him; but the dainties he brought in his pocket made them willing to display to him many of the secrets hidden from the rest of mankind.

Nor did he allow these excursions into the forest to trench upon his duty at The Magpie stables. It was customary for most of the visitors who came there to blow a horn at the corner of the village, announcing their arrival; and the moment he heard this, Eric would leave whatever employment he was engaged in, and run with all speed to take the horse, or attend to the customer if he did not want to change horses.

By this means, old Toby had no excuse for grumbling over his absence, though it might extend to several hours, if he was not thus summoned back to his duty.

So the first spring and summer passed at The Magpie. During the winter old Toby frequently had to stay at home, but nobody missed him, for by that time, Eric knew as well how to manage the horses as the old man himself, and kept everything about the stables and yard so neat and trim, that no one could find fault with him on that score; and his master hoped he would soon be able to live down the foolish prejudice that was felt against him, and so be admitted to the society of other village lads, who at present only made fun of him whenever they chanced to meet.

That he was growing up a silent, taciturn, if not morose lad was scarcely to be wondered at, for shut away from his fellows as he had always been, he felt shy in their company, and rather avoided than sought them. If there was any fun going on in the village, Eric was sure to be away in the forest, where he had as many secret hiding places as the hares and squirrels, whose friendship he sought in preference to that of lads his own age, even if they would have forgotten the old prejudice and been willing to make friends with him.

There had been nothing to awaken this prejudice against him personally until the winter was nearly over, and it happened one day that a horse was brought back to the stable in a very bad condition.

It had been over-driven, and a wound that had long since

healed had been re-opened by the hard usage he had received during the few days he had been away from Eric's care. Tyler himself was the first to remark the broken-down condition of the poor animal, and when he called Eric, he said, "Give him a warm mash, my lad; I wanted to take him out myself to-morrow, but I am afraid he won't be fit for anything for a week."

"If you could put off your journey till the day after, I think he would be ready," Eric ventured to say, as he looked the horse over.

But the landlord shook his head.

"You don't know as much about the business as I do, my boy," he said. "All the work has been taken out of poor Peggy for a week to come, and yet I would rather drive her than any other in the stable. Mind you look after her well," he added, though he knew Eric did not need to be told this, for the pity he felt for her would induce him to do everything possible to bring her into good condition again, independent of business considerations, so that he did not follow to see what was done for her relief.

The next morning, however, he went to have a look at her, to see whether it would be better to send and get old Toby to come round and see her, for he had the reputation of being a clever horse doctor, and the plight she had come home in—covered with mud and bleeding from this freshly-opened wound—made him think Toby's skill would be needful before the horse could go out again. And he had just made up his mind to send Eric and tell him to help the old man along, when he met the lad leading Peggy slowly up and down. Her knees were bandaged, and she limped a little occasionally, but otherwise seemed in good condition again.

"Did you go and see old Toby about her last night?" asked the landlord, as his eyes took in the improvement in Peggy's condition.

"No, sir; I just rubbed her with some salve I've learned to make, and gave her a dose of herbs in her warm mash—you ordered that you know, sir," added the boy.

"Yes; but I never saw a horse pick up from a simple warm mash as this one has done. What did you give her?"

"Just a few herbs, sir, that I keep here;" and as he spoke he pointed to an outhouse, where the landlord saw several bunches of dried herbs hanging from the rafters.

"Where did you get them?" asked the landlord of The Magpie.

"Just out of the forest, sir. I saw the creatures eating them, so I knew they would do no harm, and I had heard they were good physic for men, so I thought they might do our Peggy good, for she was bad enough last night."

Eric was afraid to say that his mother had taught him the use of the herbs, for fear he should be accused of meddling with witchcraft. But he was delighted to see that his master was pleased at the improvement in the horse, and assured him that she would be able to go a short journey the next day.

"But what about that old wound? How is that?" asked his master.

"Better, sir. I had made some salve—Betty gave me the fat when the last pig was killed—and I knew what herbs to put in it to make a famous heal-all, for they cured my chilblains and—"

"So you thought what would cure you could not fail on poor Peggy's hide?" laughed his master; and he felt so pleased and proud of Eric's skill that he went indoors and spoke of it to his wife.

"Summerleigh need not be afraid of losing old Toby now, for if he should take himself off to-morrow my clever little stable lad can doctor all the horses that he leaves behind."

It was an incautious speech, and he regretted having

uttered it the next moment, for his wife said, in a tone of stern rebuke, "John Tyler, I am ashamed of you. To think that you, the landlord of an inn like The Magpie, should encourage witchcraft in your own stable is truly dreadful."

"Witchcraft!" uttered the astonished man. "Who said a word about witchcraft? I only told you how cleverly the boy had doctored poor Peggy."

"Ah, and how did he do it?" solemnly asked his wife. "Did he go and ask old Toby—a decent, respectable man—what he ought to do? Did he, I say?"

"Well, no; it seems to me he knew better how to manage the job by himself, so of course he didn't go to trouble the old man," replied her husband, in rather a crestfallen tone.

"And who taught him all this, if it wasn't his witch-mother, I should like to know?" demanded the lady, in a tone of great severity.

"Oh no, it can't be witchcraft," said Tyler, remembering the salve. "He told me he had used the salve to cure his own chilblains."

"And you believed him, of course. You would believe anything he said, because you are as mad under his witch spells as the horses are. I shouldn't wonder but he bewitched Peggy before she went away this last journey, and it's through that she seemed to be in such a plight. Of course that would account for it all, for it would be easy enough to lift a spell he had put on himself. Didn't his mother do the same thing when she wanted to sell her salves and ointment—didn't every brat in the village have a sore mouth at one time?"

"Yes, and didn't the doctor say it was because the well had been sunk too near the churchyard," retorted her husband. "Mrs. Hunter had nothing to do with that, she only tried—"

"To bewitch everybody and everything that came near her," interrupted his wife, growing more angry every moment. "I believe now she laid her spells upon you before she died, and that is why you had to take that boy in Toby's place," she added, actually bursting into tears as this thought suddenly occurred to her.

With his wife's words came the recollection of what Eric had said when he went to the cottage to ask him to come. What could the lad have meant by asking if he was God's messenger whom he had been told to wait for? Tyler was by no means free from the superstition of the time, and it might be that, all unknown to himself, he had been sent to befriend this lad; and the bare suspicion of such leading on the part of another, exercised upon himself, made the man shudder, he knew not why.

Yet he sometimes repeated the well-known formula, "Lead us not into temptation"; but it was only a formula, or at most a mystic charm, and by no means words of truth to live by and seek help from, as they were to Eric himself, as he had learned them from his mother.

So, leaving the matter in this unsatisfactory condition, the landlord went to serve a customer, while Mrs. Tyler went to Betty with the tale that their stable boy had began to practise witchcraft like his mother before him.

CHAPTER III

A FATAL JOURNEY

IT was a wet, windy day in March. The few people who had ventured out in Summerleigh had taken care to secure hats and wigs by tying handkerchiefs over both, lest they should go sailing down the village street in the mud and pools of water with which the ill-kept roads abounded. The portrait of The Magpie—a gem of art in the eyes of the villagers—swung creakingly in its frame, and the landlord, looking scarcely less uneasy, stood in the porch with his eyes fixed on a distant bend of the road.

"How is she now, Betty?" he said anxiously, as he caught the sound of a heavy footstep behind him.

"Powerful bad, master. Ain't the doctor came?"

"Not yet. I'll have out the gig and go for him myself, if he don't come soon," he added.

"I doubt whether that limb of Satan ever went near him. He knows my missis always had a sharp eye on him and his wicked ways; and if he could—"

"There, go in, Betty, you know nothing about it," said Tyler sharply; and yet, as he spoke, he began to wonder whether he had not better give in to the popular notion, and get rid of Eric before the summer came round again.

A minute or two later Eric peeped round the gateway, and seeing his master said, "Will you want Peggy this morning, sir?"

"Is she fit? This weather has been hard on the poor brutes." And the landlord sighed as he thought of the broken-down condition of his horses.

"Peggy could do it, sir," said Eric; "she picks up quicker than the others do."

"Well, put her in and bring the gig round," said his master; and then he went into the house and called to Betty, took his three-cornered hat from its peg, and his heavy driving coat out of the recess, and when Eric brought round the gig, he stood in the porch, ready equipped for his journey.

"Jump in, lad; I shall take you with me, and we can kill two birds with one stone. We shall soon meet the doctor, and then I can ride back with him while you go on and see Thompson about that harness again, and tell Wilson I shall want the oats a week earlier than I expected. You're sure the doctor said he was coming round by Leaburn?"

"Yes, sir," answered Eric.

His preparations for the journey were soon made, for he had outgrown the few clothes he possessed when his mother died, and an old coat and knee breeches of his master's supplied the place of all other garments, so that he had but to turn up the high collar of the coat, button it a little closer, draw his long grey stocking-like cap a little further over his ears, and he was ready.

Betty came to the door again just as they were starting.

"The pain be awful bad agin," she said, with a keen look at Eric as she spoke.

"I'll have the doctor here soon. We shall him before he turns off to Leaburn;" and as she spoke, Tyler gave the signal to Peggy that she might move on, the chaise lurched a little, as the wheels were dragged out of a rut deeper than usual, and then they went on as fast as the holes and water-filled cart-tracks would permit.

Horse and riders were soon well bespattered with mud and water, for the road after the winter frosts and the present rain were more like a fresh-ploughed field than the king's highway and a main road to London. It was nobody's business in those times to keep the roads in order, and so the gig went floundering through the mud and water for the first mile without anything worse happening than an occasional bump and shake, with a good deal of straining on the part of Peggy, when the gig came to a positive standstill in one of the numerous holes.

Eric had gone on foot earlier in the morning, picking his way better than Peggy could, and now, seeing how slow their progress was, he proposed that he should get out, make his way to the cross roads, and tell the doctor to come straight on to Summerleigh before he went to Leaburn, while his master went back with Peggy and the gig.

But Tyler looked suspiciously at Eric as he made this proposal. Betty's words were still in his mind, and he was determined to find out whether the boy had been to the doctor, or whether he had shirked the disagreeable journey before. He had no cause to suspect the lad, for he had always done his work faithfully, and the horses fared better under his care than under old Toby's; but he knew that everybody else suspected him of evil practices, and now his own mind was a little affected by it, although the notion of its being witchcraft he could afford to laugh at by this time.

So to the lad's suggestion, he returned rather a surly answer, and they plunged on again through the mire and water, which effectually concealed the larger boulders with which this part of the road was liberally strewn.

"We must be careful here, master," said Eric, when Peggy came to a standstill before some obstacle which was hidden from sight by the sea of mud and water.

"Of course we must," said Tyler impatiently, and he gave Peggy a flick with the whip as he spoke.

The horse started forward, the wheel struck against one of the large stones, and the next minute the chaise was lying on its side, and Eric found himself in the hedge that skirted the roadway. His master lay motionless a few feet from the overturned gig, while Peggy kicked and plunged to be freed from the broken shafts and harness.

As soon as he could scramble out, Eric ran to soothe the frightened horse, thinking his master would set things straight and send him on now for the doctor. But to his dismay, Tyler never moved, never uttered a groan, though it was some minutes before he could make the horse stand still.

As soon as he had managed this, he ran to his master, and raised his head, which he found resting upon a large stone. Blood was flowing from the forehead, and Eric grew more alarmed as he noticed the deathly whiteness of the face.

"Can't you speak, master? Can't you tell me what to do?" he said in an agonised tone; and then he put his hand upon the cold lips.

They were growing stiff, and the boy, recalling his mother's death, felt sure that his kind master had received his death-blow.

He burst into tears, as he thought of the kind words he had so often received. The only really kind words that had been given him by anybody except his mother had come from this man, and now he was dead. Eric seemed to know it beyond a shadow of a doubt before any one else came near to confirm it.

How long he sat with his master's head propped upon his knee, he did not know, but presently a shout to move out of the way made him look up, and he saw the ruddy face of the old doctor, mounted on his horse, but without his gig, only a few feet from him.

"What's the matter here?" he said. "Ain't you the boy from The Magpie?"

"Yes, sir, and this is my master. We were coming to fetch you when the gig tipped over."

"Your master ought to know better than to bring a gig out in such weather," said the doctor in a grumbling tone, as he dismounted and picked his way round to where Tyler was lying.

"This is an awkward place to examine him properly," said he, after feeling the man's pulse; but Eric noticed that the doctor spoke in an altered tone, and he had turned pale while feeling his pulse.

He looked at Eric, and then at the broken chaise.

"How can we get him home quickly?" he said in a puzzled tone.

"Couldn't we carry him if I took this gate down?" said Eric, pointing to one that had been well-nigh torn from its post by the recent gale.

Fortunately a man from the neighbouring farm came in sight the next moment, and Eric shouted to him to come to their assistance.

"Why, it be the landlord of The Magpie, surely," said the man, "and he be dead too. Who did see him die?" he asked suspiciously, looking from Eric to the doctor.

"Come, help us to move him; we may lose the chance of doing anything for him, if he stays here any longer," said the doctor, without replying to the man's question.

And thus commanded, he helped Eric take down the gate, and then, when a bed of their coats had been spread on it, the injured man was carefully lifted up, and the doctor prepared to take his share in carrying him home. But before they had gone many steps, another man appeared, who took the doctor's place, and so he mounted his horse and rode forward to prepare Mrs. Tyler for the return of her husband.

The travellers had not been gone very long as it seemed to Betty before the doctor rode up, and she was beginning to describe her mistress's symptoms, when he said,—

"Yes, yes, the boy told me she was very bad when he came this morning, but she always has a fit of the megrims about this time. Something worse has happened now, I'm afraid. Where is your mistress? She must get up, if she is in bed."

"Oh, doctor, what can you mean? You know how the poor thing suffers." And Betty began to cry; but the rough old doctor went straight upstairs and told Mrs. Tyler that her husband had been thrown from his gig and seriously hurt.

"I suppose it's only the megrims again that ails you," he added.

Whatever it might be, Mrs. Tyler was ready to help when they carried her husband upstairs and laid him on the bed; only the doctor told her he must see to him first, and sent for a neighbour to give him what help he needed. But somehow, before a word had been spoken as to what the doctor feared, the neighbours knew that the landlord of The Magpie would never walk up the village street again, and when at last the announcement was made that he was dead, men and women looked at each other, and with a sagacious nod whispered,—

"I told you so; I knew how it would be when he was so obstinate about keeping that limb of Satan about the stable."

"But the horse threw him out of the gig," said another, "and his head struck one of those great boulders in the road."

"Ah! But that boy was with him, and the horse that he had bewitched did all the mischief," said a friend of old Toby's, who strongly resented Eric's doctoring the horses.

"Well, now, I've just heard he's more of a Methodist than a witch," said another; "for my Jack caught him once kneeling down in the forest saying his prayers, which is just what they Methodys do, I have heard."

"Very likely; but where is the difference, pray, when they are both agin the Church and the parsons? At all events, here's the landlord of The Magpie goes out well and hearty with this lad, and soon afterwards the doctor comes along and finds him stone dead. It'll be a case for the coroner, and twelve of us 'll have to sit on the body. Now what are we going to say about that boy?"

"What will the law allow us to say?" asked the parish clerk, who joined the group at this moment.

"That's the question we've got to consider, Mr. Jackson. Will the widow keep him on here at The Magpie, do you think?" he asked.

"He ought to be took before the justices," said another.

"He'll have to tell all he knows to the coroner."

"He's told Bill Newman and the doctor all he knows," put in another speaker; but it was evidently a gratification to all of them when the parish constable arrived and took Eric under his charge.

This was done at the doctor's suggestion, and was not unkindly meant on his part, for he had heard enough from one and the other to make him decide that the only safe place for the lad at this time was the constable's cottage. He could be kept there in safety until the inquest was over, but here in the village, when a little more ale had been consumed, some of the more brutal and reckless of the mob would probably try the experiment of ducking him in the overfull horsepond, thus adding murder to the present accident.

Poor Eric was full of trouble at the untimely death of his only friend, but there was no time for him to indulge his grief. As soon as his master had been carried home, he went back to fetch the horse and broken gig, and the latter was not an easy task, and took him some time to accomplish.

He had just got within sight of The Magpie, wearily plunging through mud and water, dragging the wrecked chaise behind him, when the constable laid his hand upon his shoulder.

"You must come with me, my lad," said the man.

The boy started and turned pale, and visions of men hung in chains for murder rose before him. "What have I done?" he gasped.

"That's just what we mean to find out," said a man who stood near.

"You go quietly home with the constable, my boy," said the doctor, who came out of The Magpie parlour on purpose to say a word to Eric.

The widow was in hysterics now she had been told the news about her husband, and really needed the doctor's care; but he was concerned for the poor boy who had happened to be the dead man's companion on that unfortunate journey, for he knew the popular opinion concerning him.

"Why should I have to go with the constable when I am wanted at the stable? Who will see to Peggy while I am away?" asked the lad.

"Never mind Peggy; she will be taken care of, never fear," said the doctor.

"Somebody ought to give her a warm mash at once," said

Eric, looking tenderly at his four-footed friend, who stood shivering in the bitter wind, but did not know whether she ought to seek the shelter of the stable, if Eric did not take her there.

This same bleak wind made the constable impatient.

"You'll have to come, you know," he said rather roughly; "for Mrs. Tyler won't have you again, and has told me to arrest you as a beggar if you do not go quietly."

So poor Eric, feeling sadly depressed and apprehensive of what might happen next, went home with the constable, who took pity on him, and gave him an old suit of clothes to wear while his own were drying, and for lodging let him have a loft over his own kitchen, which was warm and dry, if not very cheerful.

Of course there was a good deal of excited talk over Tyler's accident, and but for the doctor's care, Eric might have found himself much worse off than in the constable's loft, for all the old tales talked of during his mother's lifetime were revived now, and Summerleigh was ready to believe that the landlord of The Magpie had died from magical arts, though the verdict of the coroner's jury upon the doctor's testimony could only make it accidental death, and there was no longer any excuse for keeping Eric out of the way.

He of course had to appear before the coroner's court to be questioned and cross-questioned as to what had happened during that morning when his master met with his death, though he had told the story to one and another half a dozen times over at least.

Mrs. Tyler took care to see him before he went into the room, to let him know that he need expect no help from her. "I have got another stable boy—a respectable lad, whose mother was an honest woman and not a witch," she added.

So Eric knew that when this ordeal was over, he would be a homeless waif for whom no man cared in all the wide world. That he would be free however, to go where he pleased he had no doubt or until, when the little crowd was moving away, he was again laid hold of by the constable.

"The justices have ordered it this time," he said, in answer to the boy's appealing look.

"But what have I done?" asked Eric.

The man scratched his head. "You have no employment, no means of living, and so in the eyes of the law you are a beggar and vagabond; some say you are a poacher too, and that looks very black against you," said the man, trying to speak severely.

"Poaching?" repeated Eric. "What need had I to do that? My master always took care that I had enough to eat, and I was too fond of watching the gambols of the creatures to want to kill them."

"Well, you can tell the justices that, and anything else you can think of; but I've got my orders, and I must do my duty."

Not to the friendly constable's loft was he taken this time, but to the gaol at the next town; for a beggar was accounted no better than a thief in those days, and so with pickpockets and highwaymen, he was forced to associate during the next few weeks.

That the lad should sometimes lose heart and think that God had forgotten him was not wonderful, for here in the gaol, he was forced to hear that holy name taken in vain every hour of the day; so that to think that his mother could be right when she said God cared for every soul He had created, seemed hard of belief just now.

His habit of quiet thought and silent musing saved him a great deal now, for he was soon declared to be a poor milksop by those who sought his company at first, and he was left to himself, while the older thieves instructed the younger ones how to carry on fresh robberies when they were released.

CHAPTER IV

ENGLISH SLAVES.

LIMEHOUSE HOLE in the last century was a place of some importance, for from this port wherries for Tilbury, Gravesend, and other places started with goods and passengers, to meet the larger vessels bound for distant shores.

A few weeks after the death of Eric's master, a party of weary, woe-begone travellers arrived at Limehouse Hole, under the charge of several gaolers, for they were all prisoners under sentence of transportation to His Majesty's plantations of America. Here they would be sold as slaves to the settlers—Englishmen, like themselves, who had gone out earlier from the mother country and settled there as farmers or traders, each growing richer and more independent every year.

But in this colony, where all were masters, there was one great and ever-growing want among them—servants, or slaves to do the harder and more menial work.

The native Indians were too wild and independent to be coaxed or driven into serving the conquerors of their land, and so the mother country found it cheap and convenient to send out every spring a few shiploads of thieves and beggars to be sold as slaves to the colonists; and this was a contingent from country gaols of those doomed to be sent out to America.

There were no very desperate characters among them, but a weary-looking, patient crowd of men and women, boys and girls, and among them our friend Eric, who had been condemned by the bench of justices to transportation as a beggar, that Summerleigh might not be troubled by him again.

His clothes were a little more ragged and dirty than when he was stable boy at The Magpie, but otherwise he was not much altered by his stay in prison, and he neither looked stupid nor vicious, as many of his companions did.

As they slowly passed along the landing stage on to the deck of the wherry, Eric noticed that a middle-aged woman stood near and looked hard at each as they passed. Something in her appearance and manner reminded him strangely of his mother, and he looked straight into the clear grey eyes as he passed; and then he hoped that she was going with them on their voyage, though why he should wish for this, he could not understand, for she did not look at all the kind of woman who would be likely to go either as prisoner or warder. But still, when he and his companions were driven to the other end of the vessel, he contrived to keep his eye upon her, and when at last the boat pushed oft, and he saw she had not returned to the shore, he felt as glad as though some good fortune had come to him.

Poor fellow! He had prayed and hoped to escape from this terrible doom. And that his prayers had not been answered in the way he had expected had made him question whether God did see and know all that happened to His children in this world, or whether the argument he heard in prison, that every man was left to fight for himself and do the best he could for himself, was not true after all.

He had reached this point, but could not quite give up all hope in God and His loving care; and now the sight of this woman's face and the tender look in her eyes made him lay hold of his old faith and hope with a tighter grip once more.

There was not much accommodation for the crowd of convicts on board the wherry, barely standing room for them, in fact, at the end where they were crowded together; but Eric, with hope revived once more, could look out how to help some of his fellow convicts worse off than himself. He had got a place on the outermost edge of the crowd, but there were two poor women close by who could scarcely stand from weakness and fatigue, and so he offered to give up his place to somebody that wanted it, if they would stand close, so as to make room for the women to sit down.

"One of 'em is your mother, I 'spose," said the man; but though he said this in a sneering tone, he contrived to make some of the others move so as to leave space for the women to sit down, and, as the rest could see over their heads if they sat at the side of the boat, this was also accorded them.

Eric did not know that his action had been noticed by any one, and was greatly surprised when one of the warders touched him on the shoulder and told him he was wanted. He was near the middle of the crowd then, and not sorry to get away from his close quarters, though what he could be wanted for he did not know, and rather dreaded to discover.

But, to his relief, he saw the woman he had noticed when he came on board watching for him as he struggled through the crowd, and the warder said, "You can try him if you like, but I must keep my eye upon him till I give him up to the captain of the vessel presently."

"Will you give me your word not to try to escape?" asked the woman, looking earnestly at Eric. "I think I may trust you," she added.

"I promise," said Eric, though he felt it somewhat hard to give it, for all along he had indulged the hope of being able to get away from this unjust imprisonment, and he supposed there would be some facility for this presently, and it was hard that he should thus be required to give up the last shred of hope, so far as this world was concerned. But having given his word he would never make the attempt now.

"I want you to help me with these poor people," she said, as they moved a little way from the edge of the crowd. "I saw you give up your place to those poor women, and I noticed you as you came on board. How old are you?"

"Fifteen next month, ma'am."

"Call me Sister Martin, for that is what I want to be to each one of you," said the woman, with a smile at the boy's look of wonder.

"You made me think of my mother," said Eric, the tears slowly filling his eyes as he spoke.

"Where is your mother?" asked Sister Martin. And she was going to add, "Why have you been sent here?" But the boy's answer arrested her attention too closely.

"My mother went home to our Father in heaven about a year ago," he replied.

"Can you say 'Our Father,' then?" asked she eagerly, laying her hand upon his shoulder, and drawing further from the crowd.

Eric hesitated for a moment. "I am not sure whether I can. I have thought He had forgotten me, or that there was no God. I could not tell which it was, and I have been very miserable."

"My poor boy, has life been so very hard for you, then? Had you no friends who could help you?"

"My only friend was thrown out of his gig and killed, and I believe some thought I had done it; for they called my mother a witch and a Methodist."

"But if she was a Methodist, surely the people called Methodists would have helped you?"

"But I would not have had their help," replied Eric, almost fiercely; "my mother was no Methodist, but a good woman who loved and served God, and taught me to believe that He was my Father, who would care for me and love me."

"And so He does, my boy. The sun does not fall out of the heavens or leave off shining when the clouds hide much of his brilliance. He shines through them and gives us light still, though we may not see his face, or be able to rejoice in the sunshine. So God our Father may be hidden from us for a time by the trouble and sorrow that we meet with by the way, but He does not cease to be our Father because we cannot hold to Him as firmly as before; and He does not cease to lead and guide us because the way is rough, and not the path we would like to take. So I think you may still say that God is your Father and Friend, my lad."

"Thank you. Did you know my mother?" asked Eric, happy tears shining in his eyes; for he had given up all hope of ever hearing such words again as those he had just been listening to.

"Why should you think I knew your mother?" asked Sister Martin in some surprise.

"Because my mother used to talk to me as you do, and I have never heard any one speak like that since she died."

"Perhaps not; but God's truth lies in many hearts, but it is mostly hidden from the world, too much hidden sometimes, and that is why some of us who are called Methodists have determined to speak out and tell other poor sinners the wonderful things God has done for us. It may be that some of the people you have met had this truth lying secure in their hearts, but it was no comfort or help to you, nor were they rejoiced to know that you too were a child of God, because you could not speak out the truth that was in you."

"I was afraid, after my master told me that if I spoke about God, people would say I was a Methodist; for you see they had said my mother was a witch, and that was just about the same thing."

"Oh no, it was not," said his friend, with a smile. "You will learn to know what Methodists are like before long. Now I want you to help me with these people. Some of them are hungry, I expect. When did you have your last meal?" she asked.

"Before we left the gaol, at five o'clock this morning."

"And now it is past twelve. You must be very hungry as

well as the rest."

"Yes, but I can wait now; that talk has helped me more than anything else could." And indeed the boy's whole manner had changed during the few minutes that they had stood talking together.

"I have some bread here that I want you to help me give out to these poor people, and then some milk. But serve the women first," she added, as she filled his hands with huge slices of brown bread, and followed him with a basket filled with similar pieces.

"No scrambling, now," she said in a commanding tone, as a dozen hands were held out, and as many voices cried, "Give me a bit."

As she had surmised, Eric could slip in and out among the crowd quicker and better than she could, so that all were soon served with something like a meal; and when the last piece of bread was given out, she led the way to where a couple of cans, holding several gallons of milk, stood covered with a sack.

It required more care to serve out the tin pannikins of milk to each, but upon the whole, they were an orderly crowd, not more greedy than hungry men and women generally are; and when all had been served, she took Eric away and gave him a meal by himself, and as he ate, he told her something of his life in Summerleigh, and the cruel, narrow prejudice that had driven him away from the place.

"Where did you live before you went to this village?" asked the Methodist sister. "Had your mother no friends who could help you when she died?"

"I think we lived in London, but mother was ill there, and so we moved into the country, that she might get better. She did for a little while, and we were very happy, oh, so happy, until she told me one day that she would have to go away and leave me; but I must wait there until God sent somebody—some messenger to help me. I thought at first an angel would come and bring me what I wanted, or perhaps some of the birds out of the forest might bring me food, like the ravens took it to Elijah, but after a long time the landlord of The Magpie came and asked me to go and be stable boy at the inn, and I lived there nearly a year."

"And he was kind to you?" asked the woman.

"Oh yes, very kind; he would not care what people said about mother being a witch or a Methodist; he always took care that I had enough to eat, and plenty of clean hay to sleep in, and I could manage the rest for myself; only I was often puzzled to know whether I had done right—whether he was the messenger of God. Mother had not thought of him, I am sure, when she spoke to me about it."

"Perhaps not, but doubtless she had prayed to God to send help to you by one of His servants, but she left the choice of this servant to God Himself, knowing that He would choose more wisely than she could."

"Then you think the master of The Magpie was God's servant?" said Eric, with something like relief in his tone.

"Yes, he was undoubtedly called to do this service for you; and in doing this, he was doing God's service, though he might not know it or intend it; and in this way all the world can be made to do the will of God, though this is very different from consciously serving Him, as we have learned to do. Now I want to go and speak to the women, but you can sit at this end of the boat, and take charge of the things that are about here."

"Can I wash these?" he asked, pointing to the half-dozen pannikins that had been used in serving the milk; for he had learned while in The Magpie stables to wash every vessel after it had once been used.

"I see you are willing to be useful. Yes; one of the men will dip the water for you, and then you can wash the cans as well. They will go back in the wherry, but the pannikins we shall take with us on our voyage."

"Are you going all the way with us?" asked Eric, with a glad light in his eyes.

"Yes, my lad, I hope to be God's messenger to some of these poor people here. It is not the first time I have been out to the king's plantations of America, and if my life is spared, I hope it will not be the last. If we have a good voyage, I hope to make two journeys this year, for there is a great demand for slaves among the colonists, and the people are better off there than in our gaols."

"Then you do not think it is very dreadful to be a slave?" said Eric in some surprise.

"We will talk about that another time; I must go now," said his friend; and so he was left to wash his cans and pannikins, and afterwards to watch the green banks of the river as they slowly glided down with the tide, for there was little wind to fill their sail, or help them along; so that they could scarcely hope to reach Gravesend, where the vessel lay that was to take them across the Atlantic, until evening.

But Eric did not mind this. He could believe that this Sister Martin was God's messenger indeed, and his heart was at rest once more. He could believe that God cared for him, and was guiding him, though it might be by the rough way of slavery; still, if his Father saw that it would be best for him to travel by this road, then he would be content.

It was not until early in the evening that the large vessel was reached, and by that time everybody was hungry again, and there were no provisions on board the wherry for them; so that it was a cross, impatient crowd of convicts that were put on board the ship waiting to receive them; and Sister Martin knew that to get these fed and safely housed for the night must be her first care.

The government made no provision for the prisoners' comfort beyond finding them what was actually needful in the way of food and lodging, and the men and women themselves often preyed upon each other, for the want of some supervision—some care exercised for the protection of the weak against the tyranny of the strong.

To give this was not the chief object of these Methodist missionaries among these people, but they took the duty upon them very often, thus acting as stewardesses in the way of looking after the voyagers.

In this duty, Eric was of great service to Sister Martin, and after the first few days out, when the people began to get used to her, they were more willing than at first to listen to what she said. That she could tell them something of the country to which they were being sent; had seen it, and knew the condition of the slaves there, made them all the more willing to listen when she spoke of that other country to which all were journeying, and of the love of the Father and Friend who was willing to be their Guide thither.

To awaken something like hope in the hearts of these poor creatures was the task she set herself—hope in the Heavenly Father's love and care even for them; and that this transportation might not mean all the terrors they had dreamed of was the next step.

That they would be sold as slaves to the highest bidder without their own choice in the matter they knew very well, but beyond this they knew nothing of the probable conditions of life to which they would soon be bound.

But Sister Martin could give them some reassuring information about this. For the industrious, and those who were willing to work, life might not be so hard as in the old country. The colonists were Englishmen, and for their own sakes, if from no higher motive, were bound to provide their servants with such food, lodging and comforts as would keep them in health and ability to do their work.

The lazy and improvident were bound to find the life a hard one, for there was no room for beggars in a community where every one on entering was registered as belonging to a certain township, and carried a passport attesting the same. This was the settlers' protection against their slaves running away from them. Within the limit of the township to which he belonged, every man was free, but as soon as he got beyond the boundary, he must produce his passport, stating who he was, and where he belonged to, or he was taken off to the nearest gaol, where, if not claimed by his former master, he could be sold again; so that in getting away from one place the man would but be changing masters.

It was an outlook altogether better and more hopeful for those who did not mind working for their daily bread, and to Eric was a positive relief, especially when he heard that there were horses there as well as in England, and as he was used to them, he would probably be bought by somebody who wanted him to take care of them.

CHAPTER V.

THE VOYAGE.

"NOW help me lift him on to the other bed, where he will be more comfortable, Eric." And Sister Martin directed the lad how to hold the patient, and he carefully followed her directions, so as not to disturb the sick man more than was necessary.

"Now the medicine. You can give him that, Eric, if I pour it out." And the bottle was carried to where there was a little more light, for only a few stray beams could penetrate the gloom here.

Eric gave the medicine and supplied the man with drink, and then followed Sister Martin to another bedside, while a woman was set to wash out the dirty clothes that had been taken from the patients.

They had only been a few days at sea, but sickness had broken out among the convicts, as it frequently did on these voyages. The Methodist sister, however, was prepared for this, and had brought a stock of old clothes and a little chest of medicines, with a good supply of soap, needles and cottons, which she could teach the women to use in the course of the long voyage; for, if winds were contrary, this was greatly prolonged over the ordinary period of eight or ten weeks.

Sickness, if not too severe in type, was rather a help to the work this good woman had set herself to accomplish among these unfortunate people, for it subdued the men, and often awoke in them, and in the women, too, latent good qualities, hitherto unsuspected even by themselves; and to keep alive these sparks of true humanity when once awakened, to make these stepping stones to higher things, was the object of her teaching.

For this, she held classes among the women, to teach them how to patch and mend the clothes she had brought with her, and thus evoke their helpfulness on their own behalf and sympathy with their fellow convicts, who were to benefit by this.

The men were set to patch the boots and shoes with odd bits of leather she had brought among her stores, and all were taught the duty of cleanliness and the use of soap and water.

Then, when the daily tasks of washing, scrubbing and sewing were over, she would gather round her all who cared to listen, and tell them of the love of God their Father in heaven, who had sent His Son into this world of sin and pain, that He might know just what human pain and sorrow were, and so be able to help and sympathise with all who sought Him.

"For us, for you and me, my friends, did the Lord Jesus suffer such trials and sorrows, and such a cruel death that we might have life—might learn to know and love and serve Him, and so be made sharers in His life and love. This alone can lift us out of the power of sin and the love of sin. I need not tell you who have suffered so sorely, that sin ever leads to misery, and that to escape from misery, sin must be given up. I know some of you will say this is impossible, and in your own strength it is, but God is ready to help you in the struggle against its power, if you will only seek His help.

"To many of you, this is a fresh start in life. Old companions are left behind, and old temptations too, and in the new country to which you are going, a new life may be lived—a life whose secret spring is hidden from the world, hidden with God, but by prayer and constant looking to Him a spring of joy and help for every time of need."

This was how the Methodist sister talked to the broken-down men and women among whom she had come to live. At first, some of them might suspect and despise her, because of the prejudice that was everywhere felt against Methodists by those who did not know them.

Even Eric was not free from this at first; but as day after day passed, and they learned to know this Methodist better, all were willing to own that she was a good woman, while many thought of her as an angel of God, as indeed she was; for by her life, as well as by her words, she taught that God is love.

From the time she asked Eric to help her give out the bread among the convicts, he had been her helper in everything she had done or tried to do for the benefit of the rest. At first, he did not like the notion of her being a Methodist; but he got over this when he found that she said very little about Mr. Wesley, but spoke as his mother used to do, and was just as eager to help these men and women as he used to be with his horses, or the creatures in the forest whenever that was possible.

He had never thought men and women could be as interesting as the horses were to him, but under Sister Martin, he was learning to help these now, and to love the work too.

It did not matter to him how menial, how difficult, or how tedious the task might be, if Sister Martin wanted it done, Eric was willing to do it. One of the men in the company was a shoemaker, and for his kindness to him while he was ill, he was willing to teach Eric something of his trade, but he would show no one else, and so Eric had to learn how to patch and cobble at the old shoes, that he might show one or two others who were anxious to learn.

It was a busy life he lived here, for every minute of it was employed from early morning until he went to bed at night, and but for the dread he felt at the idea of being a slave, it would have been happier than any time he had spent since his mother's death.

But like a black cloud obscuring the distant horizon, there was ever present to his mind the thought, "I shall soon be a slave, be the property of some man who may have the right to bid me do things I may not think it right to do." And when this thought took possession of him, he would sometimes look over the side of the vessel, and wish that by some accident he might fall overboard and be drowned. If only this could happen, there would be an end of all his trouble and perplexity, and he would soon see his beloved mother once more.

But braver thoughts generally succeeded these despairing moods; for one day he told his friend what he had been thinking of when she found him gazing into the water.

"But how would you meet God, my boy?" asked Sister Martin, looking into his troubled, truthful eyes. "If you gently slipped in and sank like a stone before your work was done, could you expect your Father in heaven to meet you with the welcoming words, 'Well done, good and faithful servant?' Would you be a faithful servant, if you wilfully threw away the life God has given to be used in His service? What that service may be you cannot tell, but you can be patient and wait for the unfolding of God's providence towards you. That is your duty, my boy; we are each asked to live a day at a time the life of little children.

"When your mother lived, you knew you could depend upon her to do the best thing possible for you, and so in like manner should you depend upon God now to arrange your life day by day. The way may be rough; it is a rough and thorny path you have been called to tread, the night for you has been long and dark; but there is an old saying, that it is darkest just before the dawn, and so I think you may fairly hope your dawn is at hand, though we may not see it yet."

In this way did the good woman encourage the lad to hope and trust in the Friend who though invisible, is none the less mighty to help, mighty to save; and so Eric resisted more and more these depressing thoughts, which he found by experience always unfitted him for the duty that lay nearest to him, whatever it might be.

It was well for him that his life was a busy one, that Sister

Martin always had something she needed to be done, either for herself or for her poor people. To do anything for the personal comfort of the woman who had given up her life to bring a little brightness and hope into theirs, was a delight to Eric, and he undertook to keep her little cabin clean, and attend upon her whenever and wherever he could lighten her labour, as well as help any of the rest in performing the tasks of work they were set to do.

His life as one of their own number could not but tell upon those who were trying to profit by the instruction of Sister Martin. Here was this lad giving his help ungrudgingly to every one who needed it, and yet he had no better prospect in life than they had, though he might have deserved a better fate.

Some of them were beggars pure and simple. Work had been hard to get at first, and then by degrees they had dropped into a life of begging, in preference to seeking work. Others had gone a step further, and added stealing to the beggary, but they knew that this lad had been deprived of his liberty before he had the chance of finding employment, merely because he happened to be a stranger, as was his mother before him.

So it was a mingled feeling of respect and pity that they felt for Eric. They had each had some chance in life that they had either lost or thrown away; but this lad had been worse off than they were, for he had not been allowed even this small grace.

That every man should have his chance in life was one of the few things they all believed in, and that their hearts could be touched on behalf of Eric on this account, proved that they were not so sunk in selfishness as their miserable condition would lead one to think.

At last one of the leaders among the men ventured to speak to the captain about this matter. "Some of us can muster a shilling or two, sir, and we thought that if it could be managed that he should be sold cheap, why, we might buy his liberty for him, and let him have his chance in life, as every man has a right to expect. Some of us have had it, and thrown it away, but this chap hasn't; he is but a boy, and if the price wasn't fixed too high, we might manage it, with Sister Martin's help."

The captain looked at the man in surprise. Of course he knew Eric well enough, from seeing him about the ship, and also from the Methodist sister's report of him; but this was such an unheard-of request that he could not reply to the man without taking time to consider what he should say about it.

Later in the day, he contrived to draw Sister Martin aside, and tell her of the man's request.

"What do you think of it?" he asked.

"That my work has borne fruit far sooner than I expected," she replied, with a tremble in her voice. "These people, I know, have a little money secreted among them; but it is their most precious possession, the one thing they hold to, as affording them hope of escape from bondage by-and-by. You and I know how vain this hope is; but as money will purchase almost anything in England, how can they know it is of little use to them here? But that they are willing to give up this most precious possession for the sake of another, proves that God is at work among them; and so, if you can do this for—for us, I would say, for I should like to help in buying the boy's freedom—I think you would be doing a lasting benefit to those who give, as well as to the lad who will receive this great gift."

"Well, I will look over the list of the prisoners and their probable value, that was given to me. You see I shall have to give an account of how I have disposed of each of these convicts, and the authorities will expect to receive enough to cover the cost of their transportation. You understand that, Sister Martin, of course?"

"Yes, certainly; you are bound to deal faithfully with the authorities as well as with us, and you know I would not ask you to do otherwise."

"Then you know this lad cannot return to England, at least

not for some years—not until he has earned such means that he can present himself as a colonist, and no longer as a returned English beggar. The law is very strict about this, I can tell you; and I should find myself in a fine scrape if the boy went back in another ship soon, and by any means fell into the hands of the justices again, as he probably would do."

"I think all danger of that may be prevented, even though the boy is free. I have some friends in Boston who would doubtless be glad to employ the boy, and I think he may be trusted, especially when he knows that he would get his friends into trouble if he attempted to return home."

"Very well, then, I will see if I can fix the price for him within the means of those who are to find the money to buy his liberty. But remember, he must be made to understand that he is only free to dispose of his labour here in the colony, and by no means to return to England."

"I will make that clear to him, do not fear. I shall not speak to him about the matter yet. How much longer will our voyage last, do you think?" she added, as she turned to walk back to the other end of the vessel.

"Not more than a week. It has been a tedious one this time; and if it had not been for you and your influence over these people, it might have been much more uncomfortable for me and my men. I shall not forget this item in considering the price to be fixed on for the lad," added the captain, as he courteously shook hands with his passenger.

There was quite a little stir and bustle among the convicts concerning their important secret. Of course there were some surly and soured enough to shun all share in the little enterprise, but these were in the minority, and by far the larger number gave what they could towards making up the necessary sum; and those who did not possess a single penny they could bestow, gave earnest sympathy, for all had learned to love the lad who thought of every one's convenience and comfort before his own.

Even the sullen and surly were willing to admit that Eric was different from other lads they had known, but they did not hesitate to say they thought him a fool for running about after other people, when he might be taking it easy most of the time.

"I shall have to work by-and-by, and so will he, I expect, if he lives long enough. Precious little rest is likely to come to my share, or his either; and so I say he is a fool for not taking it when he can get it," concluded one worthy.

Another was of opinion that Eric had set his heart on getting his liberty somehow, and had hit upon the plan of running after Sister Martin as the best way of doing it. These grumblers, however, were not numerous in the company. Most of them had learned to appreciate the boy's kindness from personal experience of it, and only longed for the time when he might know that he at least was not to be a slave.

It had been arranged that Eric should not be told of his good fortune until they came within sight of Boston Harbour; indeed, the captain kept them waiting a day or two before stating the price he would require for him. It was very moderate—well within the amount they were able to collect, by the aid of what Sister Martin contributed. She, of course, was to be his nominal owner, and in her name the bill was made out; so that before the vessel went into American waters, Eric had been disposed of to the satisfaction of everybody on board.

It was thought best to tell him who was his owner, and by what means he had thus been set free, before the bustle of landing commenced; and so, as soon as the distant town came in sight, Eric was told that he had already been sold by the captain, so that the ordeal he had been dreading all through the voyage would be spared him, though no one else among his companions could expect the same favour.

The lad's surprise and gratitude when he heard how this had been effected, and from whom the plan had first originated, was very touching. He could only express his thanks in sobs and tears at first, when told of what had happened. It was as though a great burden had been rolled away; but it was hard to believe that these poor people, who were themselves to be sold as slaves, should have given well-nigh all they possessed that he might escape the terrible doom awaiting them.

"I don't deserve it," he said, as he went round to one and another, tendering them his personal thanks, and telling them how great the boon was they had been able to bestow. "It is not the work I mind," he said; "I will work harder for being free; and if ever I can help any of you who have so greatly helped me, do not fear but I will do it."

He was too much overcome to say many words, but every one knew that they had won a friend in Eric, and one they were never likely to be ashamed of, whether they met him again or not.

They did not contemplate with such utter dismay the prospect before them as they had at first. Sister Martin had dispelled some of the dread they had naturally felt about it. She had given them hope that life might at least be no worse than the one they had left behind, and for some of them at least, the future held possibilities hitherto undreamed of. That God the Father in heaven cared for them, and would provide for them, was a thought that lay warm in more than one heart now, who until they met this Methodist sister, never used the name but to take it in vain.

Now they had learned to lift their hands in prayer, and to look up to this God and Father as a Friend who cared for them, even as these servants of His had proved that they did; for thus had they learned to interpret the lives of Eric and Sister Martin.

CHAPTER VI.

A NEW HOME.

AS soon as Boston Harbour was reached, a boat was seen approaching, to ascertain what cargo the Osprey carried, and whether she had any slaves for sale.

By this messenger, notice was sent to the town-crier, that any one wanting male or female servants could get their wants supplied at the Osprey. All would be sold by private tender, unless any objection were made against the proposed purchaser. This last condition was simply a formality, as a rule; but Sister Martin had decided that it need not be thus, where a man was known to be harsh in his treatment of his slaves.

The men and women they now had were above the average in many ways, and so there would be no difficulty in finding purchasers for them, and they could afford to wait if a man came forward who was known to be a hard master. She herself had been in the colony before, and would raise the necessary objection if she found it needful.

Soon after they came to anchor, buyers began to present themselves, and Sister Martin kept her eye upon each man as he came on board, to note his prevailing characteristics.

But these colonists were for the most part steady, reliable men, hard-working and thrifty, but not disposed to take an undue advantage of the irresponsible position the law placed them in, with regard to their slaves; and so no objection was raised against any one who came forward to buy.

During that day and the next, all the men and women who had come out from England were disposed of at good prices, so that Eric having been sold cheaply would easily be looked over. But now Sister Martin, having seen the rest depart to their several homes, had to consider what she should do with her purchase—how she should find a home and employment for Eric.

Fortunately, she had several Methodist friends in this country, and she arranged with the captain to go and see some of these, leaving Eric at the ship while she went. The cargo had yet to be unladen and disposed of, and in this work, the lad would find something to do; and the captain promised to pay him for his work, if he found him steady and trustworthy.

With this money and a little further help from his kind friend, Eric hoped to be able to buy a serviceable suit of clothes before he finally left the vessel, and so he was glad to be left behind, while Sister Martin went to pay her visit into the country.

All that he had seen of the place thus far disposed him to like it, and the people too. They were a little stiff and formal, perhaps, not so free and easy in their manners as his old master at The Magpie, and they spoke with a peculiar intonation; but still, that it was his native tongue in any form that was spoken in this distant country was something to be thankful for, and that they were not so disposed to resent the intrusion of strangers among them as the people of Summerleigh were, was also another cause for thankfulness.

So Eric worked with a will among the sailors and labourers, ready to help anybody or do any one a kind turn if he had the power, while the bales and chests were lifted out of the hold and carried to the shore. To be everybody's helper and servant was not an enviable position, and before night, Eric was tired out serving his many masters, so that when he saw Sister Martin come on board at the end of the third day of his service, he was glad to welcome her, and still more glad to hear that she had found employment for him a little way out of the city.

"My friend has a great many horses, and just now is in want of a careful lad to look after some of them, and when I told him how fond you were of the creatures, he agreed to take you at once, and to pay you good wages, if you suited him. But he is particular, Eric, very particular, as most good Methodists are. I have told him the story of your life, and I am sure he will be kind to you; but still, I could see he would like you to declare yourself a Methodist and join his class meeting."

Eric shook his head.

"I could not do that at once," he said.

"Don't you think you would like Methodists?" asked Sister Martin, in some surprise.

"I am not sure; I have not seen any one but you, and I have not thought of you as a Methodist. You have been as my own mother to me. I could not expect everybody to be like you, and so I want to see first what the common sort of Methodists are. I have thought about it since you have been gone, for one of the men who came to work on the ship here said he was a Methodist. He did not seem to be ashamed of the name, as people are in England. But though he said this, he shirked his work, I noticed, whenever he could, and wanted me to help him more than I did anybody else."

"And you think he may be a common sort of Methodist?" said his friend, with a smile.

"I don't know; but that is not the way my mother taught me to love and serve God. And so I should not like to call myself by a name I should be ashamed of afterwards. You see, this is something that is closer to me than anything else. I promised the landlord of The Magpie not to speak about God to anybody; but I also told him He was more to me than anything else in the world, and so I should still think of Him and pray to Him."

"But, my dear Eric, my friend would not even want you not to speak of God. Indeed, he would want you at the class meeting to do so. Methodists are a society of people who have banded themselves together to serve God and hold themselves aloof from the world that lieth in wickedness."

"Oh yes, I heard all that from the Methodist who was working here; but it seemed to me that laziness was the thing he ought to avoid, but being a Methodist didn't seem to make much difference. I dare say he would have been lazy anywhere."

"I daresay he would," answered Sister Martin; "and it may be the man is trying to overcome this fault just because he is a Methodist; but you do not see these efforts he is making—you only see the failures. You must not expect Methodists or any other set of people to be perfect. The very fact that they band themselves together for mutual help and encouragement is a confession that they are not, but are trying to follow in the footsteps of the Lord Jesus Christ.

"Your mother was a good woman, living all alone, as it seems; but if she had gone to a place where there had been a few Methodists, and had joined them, she would have had friends ready and willing to help you when she died, and thus you might have been spared many trials and temptations. That God could and has led you in a very wonderful way to this place of safety, proves that as He fed His prophet of old by means of ravens, so He can lead and provide for His children now by the most unlikely methods. But if they can join themselves to other Christian people, and thus give them the opportunity of helping them in their time of need, they ought to do so. This is another reason why I should like to see you join the Methodists here before I return to England.

"In a few days I shall have to leave you among strangers; you may be ill, or find yourself in some trouble, needing the help of friends; if you join our society, every Methodist brother and sister is bound to help you in your hour of need; but if you choose to stand alone, I do not say you will not find friends, but you will not have the same claim upon them that you would have if you joined the society."

Eric sat silent for a few minutes after this.

"Thank you very much for what you have told me," he said; "you know I would do anything I could to please you, because you have the right to command me in anything; but still, I should like you to give me a little time to think about this."

"You know, Eric, the world at large is opposed to God and His servants; this is why the name of Methodist has come to be so hated by them. Mr. Wesley saw this long ago, and that was why he founded his society. Union is strength, and one can help another to be firm and faithful, and in time of trouble it becomes the duty of one Methodist to help another as far as he possibly can, and especially where it is needful to help him in the time of persecution, such as we often experience in England."

"I will join this society if I can, do not fear; but I cannot, even to please you, unless—"

"Unless these Methodists please you?" interrupted Sister Martin.

"No, not that exactly; but I must have time to think about it, and to see and hear them before I decide," replied Eric.

"They will not seek to control your belief beyond what is necessary."

"It is not that; I have not thought of that. But you see I must find out more for myself before I want to be called a Methodist."

From this position Sister Martin could not move the lad, though she tried several times in the course of the next day. She knew her friends would be disappointed that Eric refused to cast in his lot with the people of God; for this was how they would regard his refusal to join their society, she feared.

But still, nothing she could say was sufficient to remove his objection to declaring himself a Methodist; and so they set out the next day on their long walk to the farm, that lay some distance beyond the city of Boston.

Eric, in a new colonial suit of clothes, looked very different from the lad who had come on board the Osprey, ragged and dirty and half starved; and as the two walked together along the country road, Sister Martin could not help feeling proud of her young pupil.

After an hour's steady walking, they came within sight of her friend's farm, and she told Eric that the fields they now saw belonged to his future employer.

"Oh, look at the horses!" exclaimed Eric, in a tone of delight; for here, in the place of cows and sheep, with which the other farms had been liberally stocked, horses seemed to roam about at their sweet will.

"You will have horses enough here to please you," said his friend. "Mr. Consett supplies all the country round with horses, and takes them in to nurse when they are sick or growing old."

Eric was obliged to stand still and admire this paradise for the creatures he was so fond of. "If only my poor old Peggy could be here now!" he exclaimed, with a sigh. And then he told Sister Martin how he had learned to doctor Peggy the previous winter, and the suspicion it raised against him.

"You had better not try doctoring the horses here without consulting Mr. Consett first; but I am sure he will be glad to listen to anything you may be able to tell him about the matter," she said.

They found Mr. Consett looking out for them, and he would have taken them at once to the house for a meal, but Eric had seen a foal in one of the fields that seemed to him to be ailing, and so he told the farmer about this, and then the two set off together to see what it was, while Sister Martin went in to rest and have some dinner.

"I hope they won't be long before they come back," said

Mrs. Consett, looking from the window of the big kitchen where the meal was spread.

"John is so taken up with the creatures sometimes, that he forgets his own meal times until long after everything is cold."

"I am afraid Eric will not be much better, for it seems to me dumb animals of all kinds are greater favourites with him than men and women, and as soon as he came near the fields where the horses were he could talk of nothing else."

"I wish the boy was a Methodist," said Mrs. Consett with a sigh. "We have had several lads, you know, and somehow, being with the beasts, or rather going with them to the city, as they have to do sometimes, leads them into temptation, and I am sorry to say that after they have left us, they have not been much good to anybody. That is why John said he would do without a lad, unless he could get one who was a Methodist, and could be treated as we would treat a son of our own if we had one." And again the good woman sighed, for this had been a sorrow to herself and her husband for many years now, that with all the prosperity that had crowned their labours here, there was no child given them to share or inherit the farm.

The two had their dinner, after waiting some time for Mr. Consett and Eric to return, and just as it was over, the master came hurrying across the field alone.

"Why, what can have happened to Eric?" asked Sister Martin, who was the first to see the farmer coming. "I hope he has not been hurt by any of those creatures. I don't fancy he would be very careful to keep out of their way."

"He would not be of much use here if he was afraid to go near a horse," laughed Mrs. Consett.

But just then her husband reached the garden gate, and she went to meet him.

"Dinner ready?" he called, in a cheery voice.

"Dinner ready?" she repeated reproachfully. "Sister Martin

and I got tired of waiting for you, and so we had our meal without you. Where is the boy?" she asked, seeing Eric did not appear.

"Left him to look after Meg's foal; something ails her, and she wants seeing to for an hour," replied Mr. Consett.

"But he hasn't had his dinner," said both women in the same breath.

"Just what I told the lad; but true lovers of horses don't think of meals for themselves when the creatures need their attention. It is a test few can stand, I can tell you, Sister Martin," said Mr. Consett, with a quiet chuckle, as he took his seat at the table, and began helping himself to the ham and chicken.

"But the boy must be hungry, my dear," said his wife, in some concern for her friend's feelings about the lad.

"I daresay he is, I have no doubt he is, but a lad who has the making of a man in him don't let his hunger or any other appetite master him when duty calls him the other way. I wouldn't have left him with Meg's foal, the most valuable creature on the whole place, if I couldn't have trusted him. It was his own wish to be left to watch her for a while. I told him dinner would be waiting, but he evidently thought less of your dinner than he did of the creature who was suffering. I don't think he thought much of me or my opinion; it was the foal he was concerned with. As to his own stomach, that was clean forgotten for the time."

"Then you think the lad will do, sir?" said Sister Martin.

"I haven't the smallest doubt of it. A lad who can forget himself and his own hunger, to relieve the wants and sufferings of a dumb creature, won't go very far from God, whatever he may call himself. He told me as we went along that he couldn't decide to be a Methodist all at once; and I must say the news didn't please me much at first, though I liked the lad for telling me. But when we got to the field, and saw this foal was bad, everything else was forgotten but that our help was needed, if anything was to be done for her.

"I'm going back as soon as I have finished, and you must have something ready for the boy when he comes in; for of course he is hungry, and must eat, though I was glad to see he did not mean to let hunger be his master.

"That is the secret, Sister Martin, of success in everything, I don't care what it is; if the man or boy is master of himself, instead of allowing his appetites and passions to master him, he may be trusted to choose for himself in most things. And so I have made up my mind to let this lad take his choice as to whether he joins our society or not. If he don't choose to call himself by the name of Methodist, why, I shall be sorry, I confess, but there it will end, for he is a God-fearing lad, I can see, and what I have told you about being master of himself settles it, so far as I am concerned."

"Then you will take him, Mr. Consett?" said Sister Martin, in a relieved tone.

"Take him? To be sure I will, and glad to get him, too. The old country turns out a pearl now and then with the supposed rubbish she sends to us as slaves, and this lad is one, or I am greatly mistaken; and living here opens a man's eyes, I can tell you; so that I am not often wrong in the judgment I form of the lads who come to me. I have bought one or two, as I might have bought this lad, but when they have run away because I was too strict with them, I have not thought them worth the expense of the town-crier going after them, they were of so little service to me."

"What became of them then?" asked the visitor.

"After spending a few days in the wood, where they were nearly starved, they would come back and ask to be forgiven, generally; but I soon found an opportunity of sending them elsewhere, for horses are ticklish beasts, and need a deal of care and watching when they are out of sorts, and very few ever learn this sufficiently to be of any use; so you may judge when this lad begged to be left to watch the foal for an hour, whether I am likely to part with him in a hurry."

It was evident that Mr. Consett had taken a great liking to Eric, and Sister Martin could but feel thankful that the responsibility that she had assumed for a time had thus been taken from her shoulders so easily. But still, she wanted to know what Eric himself thought of his master, and the place where the next few years of his life at least would have to be spent. And so, when he came back from the field to have his dinner, she was very glad to be left alone with him for a little while.

"The foal is better now," he said as he came in.

"Come and get your dinner, and tell Sister Martin all about it, while you eat it," said Mrs. Consett. And when she had set the dinner on the table she left the two by themselves to talk.

"So you think you will like this place, Eric?" said his friend, when his hunger had been somewhat satisfied.

"Like it? Oh, Sister Martin, if you could see the beautiful horses Mr. Consett has got here. Little things some of them are, that want looking after carefully too. There is nothing in all the world that could be to me what the dear dumb things are, and to think I shall have these to look after and take care of. How good the Lord has been to me! I can believe now that the landlord of The Magpie was God's messenger, for it was there I learned to know so much about horses, and I also had time to go into the woods and watch the other creatures as well. Yes, he might not know it himself, but my dear old master was God's messenger, and this was the best place I could have come to, though I thought it very dreadful to be sent away as though I was a thief, just because I was poor and had nothing to do; but I see now God knew better than I did what was good for me, and I don't think I shall ever doubt Him again."

CHAPTER VII.

A WILD GOOSE CHASE.

CONSETT FARM was a notable place in its way, and the well-to-do farmer was highly respected in Boston. That he was a Methodist was something to laugh over among those who had known him before, but anything in the way of persecution, such as the followers of Mr. Wesley met with in England, was unknown in America.

But although persecution would not have been tolerated for one moment among the liberty-loving colonists, there was another way of making these people feel that they were unpopular among the giddy and thoughtless throng, and that was by trying to get the lads he employed to join in some wild adventure whenever they went into town.

"Consett's lads" were always well-known figures in the streets of Boston, for they generally led a little crowd of well-groomed, sleek-coated horses, that had either been out to the farm to recruit, or were horses recently bought by customers and brought to The Old Bell tavern for delivery to their various owners.

Now, to get the lad in charge of them, make him half tipsy, and then go off with one of the horses for an hour or two, or induce him to send the horses to the wrong owners, was a favourite device of some of the idle wights of the city, as well as of those who ought to have known better.

There was no particular ill-will felt against master or man, only Mr. Consett was known as a Methodist, and very particular, and so fun at his expense, or that of his servants, was more piquant than that which could be got out of any one else.

Eric was told of this before he had been at the farm long,

and at the same time was informed that he would have to go to the city with his master the following week, to take some horses to The Old Bell yard, and to bring home some packages which Mrs. Consett needed for her housekeeping.

Eric smiled at the tales he heard about the tricks that had been played upon his predecessors, but at the same time felt sure no one would catch him loitering or drinking when he ought to be attending to his master's business.

They set off on their journey soon after breakfast one bright summer morning, and Eric was not a little elated to find himself mounted on a spirited little pony in charge of half a dozen other horses, tethered one behind the other, and fastened to his own saddle. Mr. Consett had as many under his charge, and led the way along the road, while Eric as proud and happy as a king, followed at a short distance, wondering as he went along whether the Osprey had sailed yet, or whether he might see his dear friend once more in the streets of Boston.

She had left Consett Farm to stay in the city, that she might be at hand whenever the Osprey should have made up her cargo and be ready to sail. She also hoped to see some of those who had come out with her, that she might have an opportunity of saying a word to them of comfort and cheer in their new and strange surroundings.

Eric knew about this, and hoped that the Osprey had been detained longer in the harbour than was expected, that he might have an opportunity of seeing this dear friend once more before she sailed for England.

Mr. Consett knew all about this, and when they reached The Bell yard, and found that only two of the expected customers were waiting, he said to Eric, "You will have to stay here while I go up to the barracks with these horses, and look at one or two others belonging to the British officers. I may be detained some time, so if Treve and Mason come for their beasts, you can hand them over, and then go and look for Sister Martin.

Go to Chestnut Street first, and then inquire if the Osprey is still in harbour; for she said she might have to sleep on board the last night or two of her stay. Now you will be careful not to give up the horses to any one but the rightful owners," added Mr. Consett, as he gazed round the yard to see whether there were any loungers about, likely to lead the lad into mischief.

But for a wonder the place seemed to be deserted this morning, which so far satisfied Mr. Consett, that as he mounted his own horse once more, he called out, "Be sure you get back here by four o'clock, if you go to the Osprey; I will meet you at that time."

And then he cantered down the street, with his horses following.

After he had gone, Eric had time to look round this stable-yard, and found it much larger and altogether more imposing in appearance than that of The Magpie, though at present there did not seem to be much business going on, there were so few people about.

But presently a young fellow came out of one of the stables, and looked first at the horses, and then at Eric himself.

"Consett's lot, I suppose?" he said, with a nod.

"Yes," replied Eric; "I am waiting here to see Mr. Mason, who has bought two of these horses."

"You're a Methodist, I suppose, like Consett himself?" said the other.

"No, I am not," replied Eric; and he felt rather proud that he could say so.

"I wonder you can get on with Consett, then, if you stick to your own opinions about things; for I know he don't allow anybody to think for himself outside Methodist lines."

"Oh, he will allow me that liberty," said Eric proudly.

If he had been looking at the young man's face just then, he would have seen a peculiar smile part his lips as he said,

"Oh, well, not being a Methodist, and under Consett's thumb, you can have a glass of small ale with me, just for friendship's sake, for we shall often be able to do each other a good turn, I expect, when you are waiting here for Consett's customers."

Eric hesitated for a moment about this, but the young man went to fetch the ale while he made up his mind what he ought to do, and when he came back with the foaming tankard in his hand, Eric thought he had no further choice in the matter.

Having drunk to their future good fellowship, Eric thought he had done enough, but the young man pressed him to drink again and again, and he, not liking to seem churlish or afraid, followed his example, drank more than he had ever done before, and of stronger ale than was brewed at the farmhouse.

Presently another young man came in, and without seeming to notice Eric, asked the other if he knew whether Consett or his lad were coming to town. "There's a sailor from some ship in the harbour been asking about them; she sails to-morrow, and there's somebody aboard that wants to see Consett's lad," he went on.

"Where is the sailor?" asked Eric quickly, and running to the gateway to look down the street.

"Oh, he's gone; he was in a hurry, he said, for if they could get all the cargo aboard before the next tide, the captain said he wouldn't wait till the next day."

"That's just like Captain Simpson, and I shall never see her again!" exclaimed Eric, in a little fever of dismay. He was excited by the ale he had drunk, and the thought of being so near the Osprey, and yet not able to see Sister Martin once more, well-nigh drove him wild; and the questions and exclamations of the two young men were by no means calculated to calm him and give him a right judgment in the matter.

To go down to the harbour, take a boat, and get on board the Osprey for a parting word with his friend, and let Captain Simpson see how well he was looking, became the one thought and desire of which he was capable, and to gratify which he was ready to do almost anything.

He did not know that this was the work of the two pretended friends, who had coaxed and flattered him for this very purpose, so that now he was like an instrument in their hands, which they could easily use for the purpose they had in view when they first began the talk with him.

As soon as it suited them to do so, one of them proposed that the horses should be left in charge of his friend while he went down to the harbour with Eric.

The one who had first spoken proposed to take them under his care, while he went on this jaunt, or to deliver them to the men who were to come for them.

"It's a chance you may never get again, and it's a pity to lose it. The horses are safe enough here; Mr. Consett always puts up at The Old Bell, so you may as well go off and enjoy yourself," said this new friend.

"I'll go with you to the harbour," said the last comer; "you're a stranger, and may easily lose your way."

And as he spoke he gave the other a look which, if Eric had seen, he must have known that some mischief was intended.

But with the ale and under the urging and artful insinuations of these two, Eric thought of nothing but the getting away for a few hours, and so he soon agreed to the proposal, and the two started out.

"How far is it to the harbour?" he asked, as his guide led him down a narrow street, which he said was a short cut to the other end of the town.

"Not more than a mile. We shan't be long getting there," he added.

But they were a long time, or it seemed so to Eric, as they turned first one way and then another. But at last they did come in sight of the quay, and then his companion said,—

"There you are, my hearty! Now you can find your way, or shall I speak to one of the boatmen for you?"

"Oh, see the boatman, and ask him if he knows where the Osprey is lying now. She was over there when I left her."

"Oh, she may have been in half a dozen places since then; but one of those fellows over there is sure to know where she is to be found." And as he spoke, he pointed to a group of boatmen, and then ran across to where they were standing, slowly followed by Eric.

The bargain had been made when he joined them, and his friend said; "You're all right now; she lies a little way out, ready for sailing, but this man can take you to her." And with that, he nodded and left Eric to get into the boat by himself, while he returned to The Bell by a much shorter route than that by which he had come.

The tide was running into the harbour, and it was hard work and took a long time to go to the outer side of it, but a vessel was reached at last, and the man said, "Here we are; this is your ship."

"But I don't think this is the Osprey," said Eric, looking up at the vessel that was near them.

"The Osprey!" repeated the boatman. "You said you wanted the Dolphin, and here she is."

"Oh, but this is not the ship I want; my friend must have made a mistake," said Eric, looking all round, in the hope of seeing the vessel he thought he should know so well.

The man looked at him very hard. "Do you know what ship you do want?" he said crossly.

"Yes, the Osprey; I am quite sure of the name, and I thought my friend had told you."

"You're a fool, or your friend is, to come on a wild goose chase like this. You'll have to pay me for the time, I can tell you. Do you know where the Osprey lies?" called the boatman to one of the sailors who looked over the side of the Dolphin at this moment. There was no mistake about her name, there it was painted as plainly as paint could make the letters.

"The Osprey?" repeated the sailor. "She lay over there a few days ago." And he pointed over to where a crowd of masts stood out clear against the sky.

So the boat was turned in the direction indicated, and the boatman rowed away, grumbling, with his passenger feeling very uncomfortable. After a time these other vessels were reached, and again the Osprey was asked for, but no one knew anything about her at all here.

"The next time you come out on a fool's errand don't ask Tom Higgins to go with you," said the surly boatman at last, turning his boat towards the shore, and giving up further search for the vessel. "I shall want a crown of you, young man," he went on.

"Then it's no good going back until we do find the Osprey," said Eric in a fright. "I haven't got so much money as that, but if we find the ship, I can get it, I daresay."

Under this stimulus, the boatman made a detour round the harbour, which occupied nearly an hour; but, alas, there was no Osprey to be seen, and the man was more ill-tempered than ever before the shore was again reached, for the wild goose chase would expose him to the ridicule of his rivals, which would be as hard to bear as the loss of the money itself to a man like Higgins.

"How much money have you got?" he demanded, as Eric was stepping out of the boat.

The lad put his hand into his pocket and drew out a shilling and a few coppers. "That is all I have got, but I will bring you the rest the next time I come to Boston," said Eric, now wishing he had never left the horses, and feeling a wild desire to get back and see that they were all right.

"Where do you live?" asked the man.

"At Consett's Farm," replied Eric.

"Never heard of it before. I don't believe a word you say about this; you've just come out for a spree, and to get an hour or two on the water without paying for it. It ain't the first trick that's been played on me by you Britishers, but I don't mean to put up with this, I can tell you. You pay me a crown before you land, or I shall have you taken to the lock-up till you do pay."

Eric thought of his master and the horses that had been left in his charge, and turned hot and cold by turns as he looked at the man's hard face. "I have no more money than this," he said; "but if you will let me go, or send up to Consett Farm to-morrow, you shall have your money, and something over for waiting."

He spoke in a pleading, anxious tone, but he might as well have pleaded with the stones in the street as to this man, and finding that there was no more money to be got from him, he gave him in charge of the dock watchman for robbing him of his rightful fare.

The man was a little more inclined to think that Eric himself was the subject of a practical joke when he heard the whole story, but what could he do? The boatman insisted upon Eric being taken before the justice, as a warning to others against imposing upon poor boatmen, and so he was obliged to do his duty, as he said, though he might feel sure that Eric was not the thief the boatman thought him.

The Old Bell was too far from the dock for anybody to send there on the lad's behalf. The justices could order that to be done the next day if they thought it necessary. This was all the comfort Eric could get, and so, about the time that Mr. Consett would be riding back to The Bell to meet him, he was thrust into the dreary building chiefly used for the detention of drunken and quarrelsome sailors, or people suspected of theft, as he was now.

In the semi-gloom and quiet of this place, he had time to go over in his own mind the events of the day. The fresh air had cleared away from his brain the fumes of the strong ale he had drunk at The Bell, and recalling all that had happened, he wondered how he could have been so foolish as to be persuaded to give up the care of his master's horses to strangers, while he went off in search of his own pleasure.

He had boasted to his mistress that he knew too much of what went on at an inn yard to be persuaded by anybody to neglect his duty, and here he was, the very first time he went into town, accused of being a thief; and perhaps his master, with far greater reason, would think him one too, for he felt sure now that he had been sent out to the Dolphin purposely, and that it was by no means the mistake he had first thought it, now that he had time calmly to review all the circumstances that led up to it. But of course these thoughts did but increase his misery, and as hour after hour passed, his anguish of mind grew more intense.

He was a fool, and worse than a fool, he said to himself, to be deluded into leaving his duty at the persuasion of a couple of strangers who had undoubtedly acted from some interested motive in the matter. Perhaps the men had gone off with the horses now, and there would be no one to tell his master what had happened, that he might take steps to recover them.

The thought of his ingratitude and folly drove him almost mad, until at last the thought that even over this he could pray and seek God's help and guidance, came to him as healing balm, and he fell on his knees and poured out his whole soul before his Father in heaven.

He had done wrong, he had gone astray like a lost and foolish sheep; just when he felt so confident, so sure of himself, he had fallen. But, oh, the rest and comfort of the thought that though he had sinned, there was forgiveness for sin—that the Lord Jesus Christ could and would help him to conquer and overcome it, and He could bring light out of this darkness, order out of this tangled skein of circumstances.

After this, he decided that his first duty now was to let his master know where and how he had left the horses, and whatever punishment he deemed he ought to suffer, to take it meekly. That his Father in heaven could and would help him to decide aright was a great comfort to him; and at last, he curled himself up in one corner of the cell and went to sleep, and, despite his misery and the uncomfortable place he was in, he slept soundly until the morning.

CHAPTER VIII.

CONCLUSION.

"WHERE'S Eric? how long has he been home?" Mr. Consett spoke sharply, for he felt annoyed that the lad, as he supposed, had left Boston without waiting for him at The Old Bell, according to the arrangement made in the morning.

Mrs. Consett stopped her spinning-wheel at the sound of her husband's voice, and came to meet him.

"Where is Eric?" she asked, not having heard the precise words her husband used.

"That is what I ask you," said the farmer in a tone of irritation. "Where is the lad? What time did he get home?"

"He hasn't come home; I haven't seen him since he went with you this morning," said Mrs. Consett, in a tone of surprise.

Husband and wife stood looking at each other for a minute in blank amazement.

"What has become of the lad?" said Mrs. Consett. "A man came here about two hours ago to ask about Mason's horses that were to be delivered in Boston to-day."

"But—but hasn't he got them?" asked the farmer. "I left them with the lad to be given up, and when I went at four o'clock there were no horses there, nor Eric either."

"What can have happened?" asked Mrs. Consett, after a pause. "Have we been deceived in the lad?"

The farmer shook his head. "I can't believe that," he said.

He turned to the door, and called to another stable helper to take the horses he had brought back with him, hung up the riding-whip in its place, and then sat down to think.

"I was to have met him at The Old Bell yard at four o'clock, but it was nearly five before I got there, for I was hindered talking to some of the British officers, and I had to go to the store about your tea; and finding that nobody knew anything of Eric or the horses, I thought Mason and Treve might have fetched them early, and he had gone in search of Sister Martin or the Osprey. But I soon found that the Osprey sailed the day before yesterday, and so I concluded the lad had started for home without waiting for me."

"But he wouldn't do that, if you had told him to wait for you," objected Mrs. Consett.

"What has he done, then? Gone off with the horses like any common thief!" exclaimed the farmer.

"No, I can't believe that of him. Do you think any of those who have led our other lads into mischief sometimes have had a hand in this?" asked Mrs. Consett, after a lengthened pause.

"I might have thought so if the lad had not been used to the ways and manners of a stable-yard in the old country. He told me he knew too much to be played tricks with; and he has been so steady and thoughtful the time he has been with us, that it is not easy to account for this, as it would have been if he was like the others we have had."

"But you don't think he has gone off with the horses to steal them, do you?" exclaimed his wife.

"I don't know what to think. I would rather lose the horses than the lad ten times over. Mary, what shall we do?"

It was not often that Mr. Consett was so upset over anything as he was over this, and he said so.

"There's only one thing we can do. God knows all about what has happened, and where the lad is. Suppose we kneel down and ask Him to direct our way in this difficulty," suggested Mrs. Consett; and having secured the latch of the door, the two knelt down at once and poured out their hearts before God.

Mrs. Consett never knew until then how much her husband

had grown attached to the lad. How much easier it would be for him to lose the horses than the boy, she knew well enough now, after listening to his pleading with God on the lad's behalf.

As soon as they rose from their knees, he said, "I shall go back to The Bell at once. Get me a morsel of food that I can eat on the way."

"Go back to Boston to-night!" said Mrs. Consett.

And yet she was not surprised, for she knew how anxious her husband felt about Eric, and she set about getting him bread and meat cut into sandwiches, while a fresh horse was saddled for him to ride back to town.

It was nearly midnight before he returned, and when he came he was, if possible, looking more anxious than when he went away. "The boy is not a thief; I have got that comfort out of my journey," he said, as he jumped off his horse at the gate, where his wife was waiting for him.

"You have heard of the horses, then?" said Mrs. Consett.

"They were brought back to the stable just before I got there. They had been ridden hard for some hours, and were well-nigh exhausted; so that I feel sure more than one has had a hand in this, and I am not without hope of finding out in the morning. I could do no more to-night, so thought I had better ride home and tell you what I had discovered."

"But the lad—you have not been able to hear of him?" said Mrs. Consett anxiously.

"Only this, that he was seen going down towards the harbour, and I have seen some of the harbour watchmen, and told them to let me know early to-morrow morning, if they hear anything about such a lad. I must be off again at five, so we won't stay talking any longer now," said the farmer; and it was plain that he was well-nigh exhausted with his long day's work, but was not so anxious about Eric as when he went away.

At five o'clock the next morning, he was in the saddle again, and had reached The Old Bell yard by the time the gates were opened. The first person he happened to see was the young fellow who had led Eric astray about the Osprey being in the harbour.

"I hope nothing serious has happened to the lad," he said, as Mr. Consett alighted from his horse. "It isn't murder, sir, as you seemed to think last night."

"Oh, indeed! What do you know about the matter? I didn't see you here yesterday when I came about the horses."

"No, I was out in the country then," said the young man; but his manner was so confused that Mr. Consett felt sure that he could tell more about Eric than he had heard yet, and so he said,—

"Now, young man, I give you your choice—you can tell me all you know of what went on here with my lad as soon as my back was turned yesterday, or I shall have you taken before the justices on the charge of making away with him." And as he spoke, the farmer laid his hand upon the young man's shoulder in such a determined fashion, that in a fright he said,—

"I will tell you all I know, and I hope the lad will soon be found, for I never intended any harm; it was all done for a lark."

He then told Mr. Consett all that had occurred the previous day, adding, "We went for a ride the other side of Boston as soon as we knew he had gone to look for the ship, and did not get the horses back until late last night."

"So you are at the bottom of the mischief, are you? Well, I shall hand you over to the care of a watchman until I find out something about my lad." And the next minute, he found himself in the custody of one of the city watch, who happened to be near the gate.

Mr. Consett looked to his horses, and then another watchman arrived, who brought him some news of Eric. It was not the man who had arrested him for not paying the boatman's fare, but this one had heard all about it, and, having seen the farmer the previous night, now came to tell him what he had heard, and that Eric would be taken before the justices at eight o'clock that morning.

So, when the court opened for the admission of the public, Mr. Consett went in with the rest, and happened to stand near the boatman who had come to state the charge against Eric.

"It ain't the first time I have been set to row some young fool round the harbour, and then when it came to paying they had got no money," grumbled the man, as he told one of the crowd how cruelly he had been served.

"Then you mean to make this one pay, if possible?" said his friend.

"I do; I mean this one shall pay for himself and the rest too, if there is any justice to be had in Boston. Two or three hours and more was I rowing agin the tide a-looking for the Osprey. He knowed there was no such ship in port, of course."

"What did you say was the name of the vessel you went in search of?" asked Mr. Consett at this point.

"The Osprey, and the young rascal knew she had left the port a day or two before," answered the man angrily.

Mr. Consett would not enter into an argument about this, but asked what he thought the lad owed him for his boat fare.

The man stated the sum, and to his astonishment the farmer said, "I will pay you at once, if we can find an officer of the court who will take a note of the matter and order the lad's release."

This was done with very little difficulty, and when Eric was fetched, he heard to his surprise that he would not be taken before the justices after all, for the debt had been paid, and so he was free.

The next minute he saw his friend standing near, waiting for him, and knew at once who had paid his debt and obtained his release. But an overwhelming sense of shame and contrition seized him as he recognised Mr. Consett.

"Can you ever forgive me, sir?" he said.

But the farmer was too pleased to see him to think of anything but the gladness that was in his heart.

"My lad, my lad," he said, taking both his hands, "how did it all happen?"

But Eric was thinking of what might have happened to the horses through his folly, and so he said, "Where are the horses, sir? Did you find them all safe?"

"Yes, they are safe. But never mind the horses just now; tell me about yourself, and how you managed to get into this trouble."

"I am ashamed to meet you, sir, after the foolish, if not wicked way in which I acted yesterday," replied Eric, his face crimsoning as he spoke; for what Mr. Consett would think of him when he heard all the story, he dreaded to discover.

"Well, well, you can tell me the particulars later on. We will go back to The Bell now and have some breakfast, and then go home."

"Will you take me home with you again, sir? I think I should like to tell you all about it first, for you may not think I ought to be trusted again, after what has happened."

"I see it will ease your mind to give me your account of it all," said the farmer with a smile; and as they walked through the street back to the inn, Eric told him the whole story, not sparing himself in the least, for he saw clearly enough where he had been to blame, and how ready he was to fall into the trap laid for him, though he had thought he should be too clever for any one to betray him into such mischief.

When Mr. Consett had heard the whole, he said gravely, "Now do you see why Mr. Wesley founded his society, and laid down rules for the help and guidance of the people who call themselves Methodists? They all profess to love and serve God rather than the world, but he knew that the world would at once set about tempting them or persecuting them, and so, for their mutual help and guidance, he framed and laid down certain rules, much as we put up fences for the protection of weaker animals. One of these is that we should avoid the company of the foolish and ungodly.

"Now, if you had joined our society, and promised to obey its rules, when this stranger offered his friendship and his drink, you would have had the protection of that rule which you had promised to obey. Of course you might have broken that promise, but I don't think you would, after once giving it. Now do you see the help that our society gives to each of its members? When this fellow said to you yesterday, 'Come, drink with me for friendship's sake,' you could have said, 'Thank you, friend, but I am a Methodist.' If you could only have said that, they might have laughed and jeered at you, but they would have known that it was little use tempting you, as they did when they found you were bound by no such rules as we impose."

Eric sighed. "I never thought I should be such a fool," he said.

"Well, let this teach you wisdom for the future, my lad. Perhaps you were a little over-confident in despising our rules as so many props and stays that you could do without. As you said you preferred to serve God your own way and after the teaching of your own conscience, I thought it best to let you make a trial of it and see how you could get on walking alone, instead of in the company of God's people. These rules and regulations were not laid down to take the place of love to

God and devotion to His service, but rather to be the props and crutches that may help to keep us in the right path when the way would otherwise be dark and unknown."

"I had not thought of it in that way before," said Eric. "Do you think I should be allowed to join and call myself a Methodist after what has happened?"

"Yes, I do; for you are truly penitent for your fault, and I can feel sure that if you promise to obey the rules of our society, you will faithfully endeavour to do so. But now let us go in to breakfast, for I am hungry, and then I must see about getting this fellow released who sent you off on this wild goose chase after the Osprey."

"I was almost as much to blame as he was, for if I had only remembered my duty, and refused to leave the horses, as you had told me, it could not have happened; so I hope you will not punish him."

They had sat down to a well-spread table, and Eric was too full of thankfulness for his escape from prison to desire that another should be kept there; and so he was very glad to know that the young man was released before they left town.

"Now we must go back at a canter," said the farmer; "for the good wife only knows that you are not a thief, and she will be glad to have you back safe and sound again."

"What, after giving you so much trouble and anxiety?" said Eric, in some surprise.

The love and kindness of this friend was wonderful to him, for he had known so little of the long-suffering of love extended to him.

"Ah, my boy, you don't understand how you have crept into our hearts," said the farmer, as they went gently up a hill outside of the town. "I have been thinking as I came along, that we all think of the Heavenly Father very much as you have thought of us in this matter. You thought of the horses and my loss of time and vexation, but never once thought that all these would be forgotten in the gladness of having you back in your old place once more, and this because you did not understand how we love you—the good wife and I." And as he spoke, the farmer looked as tenderly at Eric as he might have done if he had been his own son.

The boy felt a strong impulse to throw himself into his friend's arms, if they had not both been on horseback. But from that moment, he felt that he knew what a father's love was, and that this friend was a parent rather than a master to him henceforth.

Mrs. Consett was delighted to see him return safe and well, for she had been haunted by the fear that he might have fallen overboard and been drowned, and so to see him come riding up the avenue once more was a joy indeed.

Eric needed no urging to become a Methodist after this—he regarded it as part of the love and duty that he owed his adopted father—and so the very first letter that was sent to Sister Martin in England told how Eric, her waif, had become a professed Methodist at his own desire.

The following season she came again with another party of slaves, but after this there was an end of sending convicts to His Majesty's plantations of America, for the American War broke out the following year, and so there were no more visits from Sister Martin. The war which began so hastily, and was expected to end in a few months to the confusion of the colonists, was not over until Eric was a full-grown man, and all memory of him as a slave-convict had been forgotten here in England; so that he could return to see his native country and the one dear friend it held for him without fear of discovery.

So, ten years after he left his native shore, he returned on a visit to Sister Martin, and to transact some business for his adopted father and the Methodist congregation to which he belonged.

People did not cross the Atlantic for mere pleasure in those days, and therefore, if business of some importance had not arisen, that he alone could transact for Mr. Consett, it is unlikely that Eric would ever have come back to his native land.

But when he had seen Sister Martin, and the friends of his adopted father, a desire to see his mother's grave and his old home at The Magpie took him to Summerleigh once more.

He went in very different guise from that in which he had left it ten years before, but still he wondered whether any one would recognise him as the Eric Hunter who had been driven away as a beggar and vagabond, unworthy even to be stable boy at the village inn.

Now he went back as a gentleman traveller, who could command the best horses and the best room at any inn where he might choose to put up, and as such he was received by his old mistress when he ordered a good dinner to be served, and the best bedroom in the house prepared for a lady who would come by post-chaise a few hours later.

He had ridden out on horseback, but Sister Martin had promised to come and stay with him for a few days in his old home, and it was for her comfort he was so solicitous, and so particular as to what room she would occupy.

He also insisted upon seeing to his horse himself, for this would give him a peep at the old stable-yard, and a chance of finding out whether his old dumb friend Peggy was still alive.

But although Summerleigh as a whole had stood still through all the years he had been away, and the landlady herself was not much altered from what he had known her, still there had been changes.

Old Toby lay in the churchyard, and not one of the horses he had formerly tended at The Magpie was in its stables now. The old doctor and the constable too were dead, and the boys he had known, and often envied, were lounging, sleepy-looking men, like their fathers before them.

But before he had been an hour in the place, he heard that the village still boasted of its intolerance and hatred of strangers, especially Methodists.

"I wouldn't have one o' them pestilent people in my house, no, not if they was to pay me double, sir," said the mistress of The Magpie to Eric when he ventured to make some inquiry about these people. "Summerleigh wouldn't abide 'em," she continued. "One of 'em did attempt to preach here once, but a good ducking in our horsepond cured him, and we ain't never been pestered since."

Eric thought he would like to try what he could do to break down this prejudice, but just now he had to think of Sister Martin, for her health had given way, and she was coming to try what the forest air would do for her restoration.

Eric told her what he wished the next day, as they slowly walked along the grassy paths he remembered so well in the forest, and together they formed a plan by which Summerleigh should be taken by guile.

Life in London could not be long for her, the doctor had said; but here, in the fresh country air, her life might be prolonged for some years, and so, as they walked, it was arranged that the little cottage where Eric had lived, and his mother had died, should be bought by him now, for Sister Martin's future home.

The owner would be glad to sell it, they had heard, for no one stayed in it long, since the witch woman had lived there some years ago.

The cottage was bought and put into thorough repair by Eric for his second mother, and before he returned to America, he had the joy of seeing her installed there, and received by the villagers with respect at least; for her connection with the wealthy gentleman who had bought the property made her a person of some importance in their eyes.

Here Sister Martin settled down to spend the evening of her days, and so to live the life known as Methodist, that these people could not but be touched and helped, though they might never hear the name of Wesley; for it was not Wesley, but the Lord Jesus Christ, who was the spring and fount of life in these people, and it was of Him her Master that she spoke whenever she could.

This method might be slow, but it was sure, and from her cottage home, Sister Martin could send and tell Eric of the changed life of one and another among his old friends, until at last she could venture to tell them who was their benefactor, and why he had sought to help them, so that "Eric the Waif" whom they had driven away, came to be a name of honour and renown in many a home in Summerleigh.

THE END